P R A I

Healing Grace f   e

This book is like having a Master's Degree in counseling at your fingertips! The Christ-centered approach used in this book is accompanied in a powerful way by true-life illustrations that prove that through Christ there is always hope. The authors have written a book that should be in the hands of pastors, Christian counselors and lay people alike. God's grace not only saves us but also heals us of the hurts of the past, as we forgive, and it also heals our relationships past, present and future.

Dr. Stan Coffey
Senior Pastor, The Church at Quail Creek
Amarillo, Texas

This book gives scripturally based, practical ways to overcome rejection, abuse, hurt and discouragement with hope and grace. Principles of God's Word are used to illustrate how to get rid of hostile and negative thinking by giving and receiving grace/forgiveness, which leads to healing and restoration of failed relationships.

Anna L. Foley, M.Ed, L.PC.
Pastoral Counselor/Wedding Coordinator
Trinity Church
Lubbock, Texas

The authors of this book have presented a practical working truth to the devastations of sin in our lives and have given us examples of how God's healing grace can be applied for healing and restoration. The Spirit, working through the authors, has not only revealed the deception and lies of the enemy in real life circumstances but also the solutions to the devastation of the deceptions. Instead of living in fear, we can live in hope. There is no hope or help apart from God's amazing grace!

Lynda Hunter
Women's Ministry
Amarillo, Texas

CONTENTS

ACKNOWLEDGMENTS

I (Larry) wish to praise and thank God for my precious wife, Carol, and for her love, patience, encouragement, help and prayers, as well as for my children, Brian, Lisa and Laura.

I praise and thank God for the prayer warriors and friends who prayed and encouraged me to write this book: Dr. Harold Olesen (Ginger), J. D. Davenport (Renate), Dr. David Timm (Paula) and Jerry Chenault. I praise and thank God especially for Dr. David Timm, who is not only a prayer warrior and friend but who also greatly contributed to the writing of the book by giving his time and his thoughts and for typing emails for me.

I praise and thank God for my coauthor, Dr. Norm Wright, who said to me two to three years ago, "How is the book coming?" When he found out that it wasn't coming along, he offered to help me write this book. Through his interest, motivation, loving concern and overall contribution, the book has been completed. His involvement, along with Dr. David Timm, has made all the difference.

I wish to express special appreciation to all the patients I have seen in counseling who have lived out successfully the principles of *Healing Grace for Hurting People*. They really made this book possible. It is a living testimony to them and a real encouragement and blessing to the readers of this book.

I am truly most thankful to God and the leading and guidance of the Holy Spirit.

It is the hope and prayer of Dr. Wright, myself and the others mentioned above that this book will bless every reader and further the kingdom of God in his or her life.

PREFACE

Praise God this book has already blessed several people. One very special Christian who was blessed was my daughter-in-law, Tami Renetzky, age 36, who read chapter 9 of this book before her death from cancer on December 17, 2006. She came from a dysfunctional family where anger reigned more than love. After reading chapter 9, Tami called me and said, "Dad, I need to forgive my parents, and I want to do that now." This was just one month before her death. Three days before her death, she said, "I'm so glad that I have forgiven Mom and Dad. I'm at peace now and ready to be with Jesus."

Another person who was blessed was a man with whom I shared a synopsis of the book. His response was, "I need to forgive my brother and sisters and I want to do that now." I prayed with him right then and there and led him through the steps to receive God's grace in order to pass it on in forgiveness to his siblings. When I briefly summarized the book to a doctor friend of mine, this friend discovered that he needed to forgive his father and proceeded to do so.

Hopefully, as you read this book, you too will be able to incorporate healing grace in your life and relationships and be set free from sin, hurts and rejections of the past and present, as well as those that will come in the future. Truly, God's grace not only saves us, but it also heals us at the point we need healing. God's grace heals us whether it involves healing us of the past and the way others have hurt us, or whether it involves healing all our relationships so that reconciliation can take place. The only way we can have closure of our anger is to forgive even as we have been forgiven through Jesus Christ. Yes, just as we are reconciled to God the Father through Jesus Christ, we can be reconciled to one another by that same marvelous grace.

As the hymn says:

> Grace, grace, God's grace
> Grace that will pardon and cleanse within;
> Grace, grace, God's grace
> Grace that is greater than all our sin.[1]

INTRODUCTION

How is God's healing grace applied to the wounds of hurting people? This book describes the process and the results, both of which require the presence and love of God. The following is a good example (all names have been changed):

Bill was on his way back from a successful series of crusades in West Africa when his wife, Pat, informed him that she would be staying with her father for a brief time. Thinking nothing of it, Bill said, "Okay."

While she was in route to her parents' home, Bill read a "Dear John" letter that informed him Pat had been living a double life. After 22 years of marriage and two daughters, she no longer loved him. In fact, Pat had fallen in love with his best friend, who was also the worship leader at the church where Bill was pastor. He had always said that his friend "had my back." Now he felt his best friend had driven a knife of betrayal into it.

A friend loaned Bill a book by Dr. James Dobson called *Love Must Be Tough*. It helped, but somehow Bill got bogged down in a cycle of anger, bitterness, resentment, depression, sleeplessness and the desire for revenge. Despite advice to the contrary, Bill attempted to drag Pat back into his life, but only saw her drift further and further from him and their daughters. Pat visited once or twice, admitted her guilt to the church elders, but she felt pressure even as Bill tried to keep the doors of reconciliation open through demonstrable acts of forgiveness. It seemed that the more he tried to show love and forgiveness the more hardened Pat became. She left again and initiated divorce proceedings.

Bill sought counseling with me (Larry) to help him mentally and spiritually process the anger and sense of betrayal he was feeling. It was then that the Lord showed him in a dream how *healing grace* was the answer to his and his daughters' anguish. The dream was quite vivid:

Bill and his congregation were in the church sanctuary, gasping for breath as smoke filled the building. Bill heard the Lord say that the smoke was revenge and anger, which was about to burst into flames—everyone must get low to avoid inhaling the toxic fumes. Everyone followed Bill's example as he relayed God's instructions, crouching low to the ground.

It was then that Bill noticed a door with a sign that read, *This Way to God's Love*. He tried to open the door, but it was locked. On the door's handle was written the word "Offense," and in the lock was a key labeled "Forgiveness." Even after Bill turned the key, however, the door would not budge.

Just then, hinges appeared on the door. Bill heard the Lord's loving voice: "The hinges represent God's grace; everything in life hinges on My grace." As Bill grasped the handle again, the door swung open. Bill and his congregation walked through the door of forgiveness and grace, leading to a sanctuary of fresh air filled with the presence and peace of God.

The next day, Bill built a door exactly like the one he had seen in his dream and preached an illustrated message. The entire church, including Bill and his daughters, passed through the door of forgiveness into God's love and grace, just as they had done in the dream.

As you read this book, we trust that you too will find God's healing grace for your hurts, just as Bill, his daughters and his entire congregation found it.

There Is Hope for You

Mary, an attractive woman with an outgoing personality, wanted to be married.[1] She never lacked dates, but her relationships never seemed to go anywhere. They'd start out well and she would have high hopes, but after a few months, they'd fizzle. She didn't know if the problem was with her or the men she chose. Did she have unidentified emotional wounds, or did they?

Judy, who has been married for a number of years, entered marriage under bondage—not to her husband, but to her father. For years her father had sexually abused and traumatized her. Her wounds were deeply buried. Gradually, her marriage moved to the point of crisis. Was there any hope that it could survive?

Ryan's decisions were based on pleasing his father. He went as far as becoming a doctor in an attempt to find recognition from his dad. Along the way, Ryan made mistakes—lots of them. He had an affair. He exhibited erratic behavior at home. His relationships with his colleagues were strained. He was filled with anger and bitterness.

Sarah had been beaten down over a long period of time; first by her parents and then by her four husbands and her own children. She attempted suicide numerous times. On the last occasion she set fire to her house and herself. The fact that she even survived that suicide attempt was miraculous; but afterward, she was lost in the shell of herself, incommunicado and alone. Was it possible that she could be drawn out of the cave of her wounded heart?

Life wasn't working for any of these people, and maybe it's not working for you either. Maybe you're asking, "Why me? Why can't my life turn around? I know other people have difficulties, but I see lots of people who don't have the hassles I do. Sure, they have rough spots at times, but my life seems to be one difficulty after another. What's wrong with me? There's got to be a better way to live. I know there is. But where is it? I just can't find what works!"

Many people are searching for answers to life. We know this is true because of the success of television programs such as *Oprah* and *Dr. Phil*, and many others, and because of the popularity of self-help seminars and books featuring information on how to "get it all together." That's not to say there isn't some good advice and material available. There is. But healthy relationships are not built on techniques or programs; *healthy relationships are built on something that changes lives.*

The *Something* That Makes Life Work

In this book you will read about people who have discovered the "something" that works. Their lives have been changed. You'll discover what happened to Mary, Ryan, Judy, Sarah, and others we have counseled. You will see that these people often relieved their discomfort by overeating; engaging in destructive relationships; exploding in anger; or using drugs, alcohol or pornography to numb their pain. They were often depressed, anxious and alone.

As you read their stories, you might swear that we have written about you. But be assured, we do not have private information on you! There are many others in this world who struggle with the same issues you do. Be doubly assured that God has *healing grace* waiting for you just as He had for Mary, Ryan, Judy and Sarah. It is because of His awesome grace that we have hope.

There is hope for everyone, and there is hope for *you*. Nothing you have done or that others have done to you is so terrible that it can keep you from God's healing grace and from experiencing healing of your deepest wounds. Nothing but personal pride and unwillingness can keep you from receiving forgiveness—*God's forgiveness*—and from releasing forgiveness to those who have hurt you.

Healing is a journey that begins when someone gives you the key to your life and you open the gate, allowing all of the pain, rejection, tragedy, hatred, anger, distrust and resentment to flood out of your heart, never to bother or enslave you again. As you step out in faith on this journey of grace, you will learn what it means to forgive yourself. As you continue to walk in healing grace, you will begin to love yourself, to love others (not just tolerate them), and to forgive your parents, siblings, spouse, friends and others who may have hurt you in the past.

Those of you who have been abused sexually, physically, emotionally and/or verbally will finally be able to forgive the man or woman who abused you. You will be able to look on those people not with disdain or even pity but with true empathy and compassion for the tremendous need they have in their own lives. You will realize that these people also need healing grace.

Keys to Recovery

We come to you as counselors. Between the two of us, we have almost 90 years of counseling experience. We want to share with you some truths that work. We didn't originate these truths; they come from God's Word, and they can change your life.

One of the keys to recovery that we discuss in detail is recognizing that the real problem is based in "self" and not necessarily in circumstances. It's true that our environment as well as negative and destructive people can hinder positive change, but the bottom line is that we have a choice. *Self* is often our worst enemy. Self keeps us locked in a perpetual straitjacket of bondage. *We* often get in the way of our own healing. Once we can get self out of the way, we can open the door of our heart and mind to the true cure for our problem, which is the grace of God and the love of Jesus Christ. "Grace" is the key word that, in addition to the six healing phrases you will learn in this book, will change your life and your relationships.

The person who *appropriates* grace and truth is the one who benefits most from them. As it is written in Proverbs, a plan in the heart of a man is like deep water, but a man of understanding draws it out (see Prov. 20:5). Counseling is mostly about the art of digging into the heart and mind to uncover past events that impact current behavior and then seeking to correct wrong patterns of thinking and feeling that have led to the undesired behavior. This is a simplistic way to view counseling, but it is much of what Jesus did to bring people to an understanding of who God is and who they could be in Him.

Jesus came to give us hope and set us free from fear. Hope and fear are two of the greatest motivating forces in life. Both of these motivators can produce life-changing results. Fear is a powerful *negative* drive, compelling us forward while at the same time inhibiting our progress. Fear is like a noose that slowly tightens when we move in the wrong direction. Fear restricts our abilities and thoughts and leads us toward panicked reactions.

Even when we're standing on the threshold of success, our most creative and inventive plans can be sabotaged by fear. We'll discuss fear—and how to conquer it—in chapter 3.

Hope is a powerful *positive* force. Hope is like a magnet that draws you toward your goal. Hope expands your life and brings a message of possibility and change. It draws you away from the bad experiences of the past and toward better experiences in the future. The hope video replays scenarios of potential success. Hope causes you to say, "I can do it; I will succeed." It overrides all of those perceptions of not feeling safe.

Jesus came to Earth bringing hope. Hope is what everyone needs. As it is written in Romans, "May the God of *all hope* fill you with all joy and peace as you trust in Him, so you can overflow with hope through the power of the Holy Spirit" (15:13, emphasis added).

God knows your situation and He cares about you. He has the supernatural ability to take you from where you are and bring you to the place where He wants you to be. One of our favorite verses says that if any person is in Christ, he or she is a new creation. The old has passed away and the new has come (see 2 Cor. 5:17).

You may already know Jesus personally and may be thinking, *Why am I having problems? Shouldn't I already be like Christ without having to go through extensive counseling?* But the reality of the Christian life is that, although we are born again into God's family and He gives us a new nature, we are still living in bodies that have been corrupted by the many things we experience in the world. In Galatians 5:16-17, Paul says that the flesh itself works against the Spirit so that we may not do what we want to do. Paul also states in Romans 12:2 that we are not to be conformed to the patterns of the world, but transformed into the people God wants us to be by the constant *bathing of our mind* with the Word of God.

A key verse to bathe your mind in on your journey of recovery will be Colossians 3:13: "Bear with each other and *forgive* whatever grievances you may have against one another. *Forgive* as the Lord forgave you" (emphasis added). Just as we have been forgiven through Jesus' death on the cross, so must we also (and through Christ have the power to) forgive others. Forgiveness is a primary key to recovery. We access it through the healing grace of God. Forgiving others as well as *yourself* will make all the difference. Sound impossible? Jesus said, "with God all things are possible" (Matt. 19:26)!

And we're here to walk along with you. There's something about having a person come alongside you and show you the truth that can shake you out of a state of self-pity and regret, anger and resentment, or pain and unforgiveness. That helping hand can lift you up to a place of strength so that you can function optimally, as God designed you. In this book, you will begin to identify with the stories of people who have overcome overwhelming difficulties like your own. You will receive hope for the resolution of issues in your life. You *can* triumph over those barriers to success—barriers that until now have led you to devastating consequences or have literally ruined your life and the lives of those around you. Remember, you are not alone. Healing is just a heartbeat away.

When Life Isn't Working

Some people feel that their life doesn't work. Maybe they feel like it has *never* worked. Some don't even realize there is a problem until something very dear to them has been taken away. That something may be a job, a spouse, a boyfriend or girlfriend, a child, or some cherished possession. For some, losing face in the community or among peers is more important than anything else and, once that is lost, they finally realize there's a problem.

We are not going to write about hypothetical situations. The examples in this book are all true. The names of the characters and some demographics have been changed to keep the actual identities confidential, but the stories are real. The people we write about have given permission for their stories to be told so that they may have a part in helping you receive healing grace.

So, is your life working?

Perhaps you have recently discovered that your husband has been viewing pornographic pictures on the Internet. You've asked him to stop, but he hasn't, so you've asked him for a divorce. You have two kids, and you've demanded custody of them. You find yourself alone for the first time in your life, unable to make a decision. Outwardly your husband is sorry and has said that he wants to work it out. He's asked you to reconsider the divorce and is willing to get counseling. But you can't go forward, and you dare not go back.

Life is not working.

Or maybe you're a mother of two and have an excellent corporate job. But none of your three marriages have worked out. You have a difficult time trusting and loving a man. You're afraid each man will be a replica of your father, who was a perfectionist and a controlling alcoholic. You vacillated between fear of him and wanting his love and approval. He wasn't available emotionally, so you tend to view all men like your dad.

Life is not working.

Perhaps your story looks more like this: Three years ago you separated from your wife after she kicked you out because of a brief affair you had while on a drunken binge. You went to Alcoholics Anonymous, got sober and have not had a drink in two-and-a-half years, and you haven't even looked at another woman. But your wife doesn't trust you. Every time you go to counseling, she slices and dices you. You have asked to speak to her on numerous occasions. She will not divorce you, but she won't get back with you. You recently suffered a major back problem and haven't been able to work, but she won't put you on her insurance, even though technically you're still married. Your wife tortures you—and herself—with her inability to let go of the past.

Life is not working.

When Mark was a child, his parents were cold, indifferent and obsessed with performance. In order to try to please them, he excelled in every intellectual pursuit possible. He was the valedictorian of his high school. He graduated with a bachelor's degree in physics and went on to get an advanced degree. He became a successful professor and department chairman of a prestigious university. Mark was even an elder at his church. Yet his wife and three kids were hurting for intimacy.

Like Mark, you may be able to teach your family about quantum mechanics and high-velocity particle physics but can't give them what you never received growing up—love and intimacy. Later in the book we will return to Mark's story and what he learned about the "secret of the universe." Before he learned this, however, life was not working for him or his family.

You may be like another man we know. Paul is a successful businessman in his 30s. He came to the office with his pastor, depressed, angry and ready to kill his wife and himself; he decided against the latter because there would be no one left to take care of their three kids. He appears to be the dream guy: wealthy, a Sunday School teacher, deacon, chairman of evangelism, and so forth The only thing he hasn't done is raise the dead! He's the envy of all who want to be "spiritual." He also has a beautiful wife with a voice like an angel. She sings in revival services everywhere and is looked up to by men and women alike. There's just one little problem. She's had affairs with pastors, song leaders and evangelists—five people he actually knew. While Paul is being the successful, self-actualized businessman, his wife is lonely and seeking ways to make the pain of solitude go away.

Life isn't working for either of them.

You understand what the words "life isn't working" mean because, frankly, your life isn't working either. Perhaps you're unfulfilled, depressed, overweight, unloved, abused, outcast. Even worse, perhaps you are a prominent man or woman in your peer group—everyone else thinks you have it together, but inside you're full of dead men's bones. You know it's all a façade. You're living a lie—someone else's idea of a great life—but it's not working for you. It's a struggle to face up to the problem(s) and to stop hiding behind the happy face. Later in this book we'll address the problem that got you where you are today and what you can do about it. We will talk about forgiveness—finding the courage to forgive yourself and everyone else who ever scarred you.

So if you realize that you are one of those whose life is not working, take a minute now to think about the reasons why. But first, give yourself the right to expect better. Believe in your heart that there is something or someone out there who can help make a difference in your life. Reject the belief that there's nothing more for you than the job, the home, the 1.8 kids, the cat and the dog. Believe that you can have a successful relationship with someone of the opposite sex. Believe that you *can* be fulfilled in life. Believe that there is a purpose other than to have pleasure. Believe that you can have joy. Believe that you will be *healed*. Seeing is *not* believing. Usually it is just the opposite. You will only see a difference when you start believing that there can be a difference.

Congratulations! You have taken your first step toward receiving healing grace by recognizing that there is a problem and the possibility, even if you think it may be slight, of a solution. Perhaps you're beginning to see that maybe you've been approaching the problem(s), or your situation, in a dysfunctional way. Perhaps you've been looking for an *escape*. That's the way many people try to deal with their issues—especially the people in the following chapters.

When life isn't working, a person will (often subconsciously) search for an escape through pornography, sex, unhealthy relationships, food, alcohol, drugs (both prescription and illegal), isolation, anger, suicide or even the façade of having it all together. These means of "escaping" pain and fear only lead to dead ends, to traps that close in and bring deeper bondage.

In chapter 2, we'll dig deeper into why unhealthy escapes don't work. They drive a person farther from the liberty they seek.

We'll discuss what it means to be in bondage—to be in a prison of your own making—and how the healing grace of Jesus Christ can set you free. He is the Author of true freedom. As Galatians 5:1 declares, "It is for freedom that Christ has set us free. Stand firm, then, and do not let yourselves be burdened again by a yoke of slavery." He desires to free us from our past and our heavy burdens. He loves and values us so much that He died and rose again to bring us that freedom.

You Have a Choice

What do you believe you are worth? Well, consider that God created us with the ability to choose right from wrong. We call it "free will." He cares so much for our freedom to choose that He will not interfere. That is true love. He wants us to choose life through Jesus Christ, to truly be a new creature in Christ so that through Jesus our Lord, we can do what we could never do on our own (see 2 Cor. 5:17; Gal. 2:20).

What circumstance are you going through right now that is causing you emotional pain? Have you blamed someone else for your difficulty? Do you wrestle with anger and unforgiveness, allowing these emotions to negatively affect your marriage, family and other relationships? Are you able to take responsibility for the problems in your life?

If you feel like you've been victimized, remember that it was *not* your fault if your parents divorced, if someone abused you, if your mother rejected you and gave you up for adoption, if you got laid off from your job, or if _____ (you fill in the blank). The way you respond to any situation, however, will determine whether life is or is not working for you. You can't undo the past with all of its pain and hurt, but you can decide today that you will no longer live as a victim of the past. You can put yourself in a position to receive healing grace today

There are forces over which we have no control that influence our life and involve us in things. The factors are variable and they change over time with the changing face of evil in the world. But one thing is constant—how we react to our environment and the people around us. *We have a choice* in how we approach a problem and how we think about important issues and relationships in our lives. The moral decline of our country may not be your direct responsibility, but you are responsible for yourself. Life is not working for much of our society, but life can work for you if you are willing to learn, grow and change.

There are many events that have happened in my life that I (Norm) never anticipated. I never expected that an office next to mine would be blown up by terrorists and that people would be injured and killed. But it happened.

I never expected a business associate to mismanage the running of my business to the extent that I would almost lose it all. But it happened.

I never expected that, on one of my outings as a youth director, a high school boy would fall over a 400-foot cliff to his death. It happened. I watched as they carried him out in a body bag on a horse.

I never expected that my daughter, at the age of 20, would take a detour in her Christian life and live with boyfriends, use cocaine and move into alcoholism. But it happened and continued to happen for four years.

I never expected to have my only son born profoundly mentally retarded with brain damage and then suddenly die at the age of 22. But it happened.

And I never expected that my wife, Joyce, would have a malignant brain tumor. But this, too, happened.

Over the years, my wife and I have learned the truth and significance of many passages from God's Word. One passage in particular came alive as we depended on it more and more: "Consider it all joy, my brethren, when you encounter various trials, knowing that the testing [or trying] of your faith produces endurance" (Jas. 1:2-4, *NASB*).

The *Amplified* version says, "But let endurance and steadfastness and patience have full play and do a thorough work, so that you may be [people] perfectly and fully developed [with no defects], lacking in nothing" (Jas. 1:4).

Learning to put that attitude into practice is a process. The passage does not say, "respond this way immediately." You have to feel the pain and grief first, and then you'll be able to consider it all joy.

What does the word "consider" mean? As I studied commentaries, I discovered that the word refers to an internal attitude of the heart or mind that allows the trial and circumstance of life to affect us either adversely or beneficially. Another way that James 1:2 might be translated is this: "Make up your mind to regard adversity as something to welcome or be glad about."

You have the power to decide what your attitude will be. You can say about a trial, "That's terrible. Totally upsetting. That's the last thing I wanted for my life. Why did it have to happen now? Why me?"

The other way of "considering" the same difficulty is to say, "It's not what I wanted or expected, but it's here. There are going to be some difficult times, but how can I make the best of them?" Don't deny the pain or hurt you might have to go through. Instead, ask, "What can I learn from it? How can I grow through this? How can I use it for God's glory?"

The verb tense used in the word "consider" indicates a decisiveness of action. It's not an attitude of resignation—*Well, I'll just give up. I'm stuck with this problem. That's the way life is.* If you resign yourself, you will sit back and do nothing. But James 1:2 indicates that you will have to go against your natural inclination in order to see the trial as a positive thing. There will be some moments when you'll have to remind yourself, *I think there's a better way of responding to this. Lord, I really want You to help me see it from a different perspective.* Then your mind will shift to a more constructive response. This often takes a lot of work on your part. Discovering the truth of the verse in James and many other passages like it will enable you to develop a biblical perspective on life. And that is the ultimate survival tool. Notice that I didn't say this is an immediate response. It takes time. The greater the loss and the worse the trauma, the longer the recovery will take.

God created us with both the capacity and the freedom to determine how we respond to the unexpected incidents life brings our way. You wish that a certain event had never occurred, but you can't change the fact that it did. But you *can* choose your attitude. There are those who choose a life of misery and allow the voice of imaginary critics to dominate their thoughts and keep them beaten down or enslaved by negative emotions; and there are those who choose *hope*. There is always hope. You must *choose* to believe that.

You also have a choice to forgive, and to believe that forgiveness brings healing. Many choose to languish in the pit of unforgiveness, allowing bitterness to take root in their hearts. In this dark place, the light of truth cannot be seen, and the one who chooses to remain in it becomes more and more self-centered, more and more bitter. You could call it self-*pity*, for it is a pit. It's one of several prisons that we can lock ourselves into if we don't seek help from God and others.

We'll go much deeper into detail on this subject in the chapters ahead. You will read about the lives of those who have been set free from self-imposed prisons of unforgiveness, bitterness, self-hatred and fear. You or someone you love might feel trapped and alone in one of those prisons right now, but please know that there are people you have never met who care about you and your situation and who want to help set you free. Even though we can't see you in our clinic or call to encourage you, we've spent hundreds of hours compiling this book to introduce you to healing grace.

The hopelessness of a human soul, the shallow look in the eye, the resigned defeat of the spirit of a man or woman are only temporary if that person is serious about healing. You need to develop the mindset that where you are today is only temporary. The future is bright for those who take hold of healing grace or, rather, allow healing grace to take hold of them.

You may have been rejected as a child. You may have outlived all of your friends and family. You may be alienated by society and living in prison. But your life is still a gift. The desire of this ministry team is to help you realize your potential and to receive, as well as achieve, God's healing grace. So join us in the adventure of a lifetime. The journey is fraught with pitfalls, challenges and enemies within and without, but when you have passed the test and faced your enemy head-on and won the battle, you will be one of the healed, and no one can ever take away your victory.

You are a victor, not a victim—a conqueror, not a loser. You are an overcomer. You're going through a refining fire and you will come out like silver. Your metal (and your mettle) is being tested and your impurities removed. Now you stand with those who have taken a similar journey. We welcome you to join them on that journey down the path to freedom and become free indeed. You will never regret it. As Jesus said, "You shall know the truth and the truth will set you free" (John 8:32, *TLB*).

CHAPTER 2

What Is Healing Grace?

B y now you are curious or wondering what grace is. Throughout the Bible the word "grace" is used in relation to *favor*, particularly divine favor or help that is not earned but bestowed as a gift. Philip Yancey defines grace this way in his book *What's So Amazing About Grace*:

> Grace makes its appearance in so many forms that I have trouble defining it. I am ready, though, to attempt something like a definition of grace in relation to God. *Grace means there is nothing we can do to make God love us more*—no amount of spiritual calisthenics and renunciations, no amount of knowledge gained from seminaries and divinity schools, no amount of crusading on behalf of righteous causes. *And grace means there is nothing we can do to make God love us less*—no amount of racism or pride or pornography or adultery or even murder. Grace means that God already loves us as much as an infinite God can possibly love.[1]

You and I are like a bank account that has insufficient funds. We're always in debt. And we end up in despair. But if we're walking with Christ, we have been saved by grace and are made alive by grace. John Ortberg, in *Love Beyond Reason,* gives a clear description of what God's grace has done:

> This is grace for anyone who's ever despaired over sin. This is the removal of our mountain of moral indebtedness. If you've ever felt that a gap between reality and who you're called to be, ever felt like you can't close it—

this is grace for you. God took our indebtedness and guilt and nailed it to the cross. He erased the bill, destroyed the IOU, so you are free. Unburdened. Cleansed. You can live with a heart as light as a feather. Today—no matter what you did yesterday. This is the wonder of grace.[2]

Grace is totally free. It cannot be bought. It is undeserved, unearned and cannot be repaid. Ephesians 2:4-5 says, "But because of his great love for us, God, who is rich in mercy, made us alive with Christ even when we were dead in transgressions—it is by grace you have been saved."

God doesn't say . . .

"I love you *because* . . ."

"I love you *since* . . ."

"I will love you *if* . . ."

"I will love you *when* . . ."

"I will love you *after* . . ."

"I will love you *provided* . . ."

In no way is God's love conditional.[3]

Simply put, grace extends favor and kindness to one who doesn't deserve it and can never earn it. Every time you think of the word "grace," think undeserved, undeserved, undeserved.

Grace is given free and clear with no strings attached.

The Transforming Power of Grace

Grace can be simply defined as a free gift from God that results in a major healing within you. First, it is healing of your sin, and it involves a healing of your past, a washing away of your hurts and rejection as you allow God to work in your heart to help you forgive just as you have been forgiven. Grace is His kind disposition, unconditional love, concern, compassion and favor toward you, no matter the circumstance—yes, no matter the situation. The greatest gift of His grace was given to us through Christ. Let the following words melt your heart:

> Because of Christ's redemption
> I am a new creation of infinite worth.
> I am deeply loved,
> I am completely forgiven,
> I am totally pleasing,
> I am totally accepted by God.
> I am absolutely complete in Christ.
> When my performance
> Reflects my new identity in Christ,
> That reflection is dynamically unique.
> There has never been another person like me
> In the history of mankind,
> Nor will there ever be.
> God has made me an original,
> One of a kind,
> A special person.[4]

You have been declared someone special. As it says in Ephesians 1:4-5, "Long ago, even before he made the world, God chose us to be his very own, through what Christ would do for us; he decided then to make us holy in his eyes, without a single fault—we who stand before him covered with his love.

His unchanging plan has always been to adopt us into his own family by sending Jesus Christ to die for us. And he did this because he wanted to!" (*NLT*).

Yet, as beautiful as these words are, they are so hard for most of us to grasp and truly believe about ourselves. Once we are in God's grace, however—once we receive and embrace it—grace begins to transform us. God Himself uses it to heal us of every sin, every sense of inadequacy, every bit of pain from our past. This is why we write about *healing* grace. We don't want you to let grace slip past you any longer as merely a religious buzzword; we want you to *experience* grace. God wants you to experience it! And not only as a one-time emotional event but as a *lifestyle*, as something you breathe and live and *give out*.

We become people of grace when we give out what we've been given. Focusing on someone other than yourself is sometimes the first step in getting over the pain of depression, loneliness and despair. Whatever you focus on will enlarge. If you focus on yourself and your own problems, those problems will increase in your heart and mind. The point is that focus on self leads to many heartaches and defeats. If you're tired of focusing on your failures and on the ways that others have failed you, then healing grace is for you. It is for you to freely receive and to freely give.

Though we wrote this book with you and your healing in mind, we also wrote it with healing in mind for those who have hurt you. As you journey through the process of your own healing, you will discover that a major part of that healing will be about forgiving others as you have been forgiven. Forgiveness is grace in action, grace that transforms. It is the grace that heals hearts and restores relationships.

The Practice of Healing Grace

"Grace" is a healing word that we will refer to throughout this book. In addition, we will also refer to the following six healing phrases:

"I was wrong."

"You were right."

"I am sorry."

"I forgive you."

"Please forgive me."

"I love you."

Carefully read these phrases, and then take a minute to write them down. Put the list somewhere where you'll see it frequently. We hope these phrases will begin to "season" your vocabulary. Over time, these phrases will become second nature to you, easily spoken in moments of need. As Proverbs 25:11 says, may they be words "aptly spoken like apples of gold in settings of silver."

Do you think you could use these words the next time you encounter conflict with someone who rubs you the wrong way? What about when you think of a parent, spouse or significant other who abused or neglected you? Perhaps that seems impossible now, but we believe that by the time you finish this book, with the grace of God and a willingness in your heart to change, you will be able to speak these words and communicate grace to even your worst offenders.

The desire to change, of course, is essential before any real change can occur. Another key to any significant change is recognizing the source of the problem. Proverbs 23:7 says, "As a man thinks in his heart, so is he" (*NKJV*). We can't put a Band-Aid on our problems and deep wounds; rather we must deal with the real problem through God's healing grace.

Our heart is prone to do destructive things when life doesn't seem to be working. By allowing the light of Christ to probe our heart, we can see what lies at the root of our destructive behavior and thought patterns. With the source of our pain and problem(s) revealed, and the grace of God available, our hearts can begin to heal. Once the heart changes, the mind can accept the truth and begin to apply grace to real-life situations.

Ryan's Story

Ryan grew up in an environment where performance was the most important aspect to life. His father communicated through actions (if not words), "I love you when you do everything I ask you to do." Jesus says, "I love you because I choose to love you" (see John 15:12-13,16).

Ryan's father got angry when Ryan gave less than a perfect performance. Jesus says we who labor and are heavy laden are to come to Him and He will give us rest (see Matt. 11:28-30).

His father got angry when Ryan was frustrated and rebellious; but Jesus waits on high to have compassion on us, and when He hears our prayers He will certainly forgive and be gracious to us (see 1 John 1:9).

Needless to say, his father's expectations led to performance-based acceptance of himself and others who attempted to have a relationship with him. It was only later, when Ryan came into a Christ-centered relationship, that he got free from perceived demands to be perfect.

When Ryan was a young man, he left home, got a job and married. He continued to struggle with performance-based acceptance of himself and others. Medical school was a chance for him to establish some self-esteem. However, the better he performed, the more attention he wanted. He continued to have problems with anger that cost him dearly in terms of relationships with his colleagues. Because he could not love himself in a healthy manner, or love others with all of their faults, he became a perfectionist. His relationships deteriorated to the point of near extinction. Faulty patterns of thinking that had developed when he was a child continued for decades until the losses he experienced multiplied.

The light bulb, surprisingly, didn't come on for Ryan even then. It was always someone else who made the error or could not adapt or was out to get him. He was the victim. He could never see the blind spot that was his own erroneous thinking and behavior. He felt that he was "normal," or at least normal for a physician. Incredibly, his wife put up with a brief affair that he had early in their marriage. She tolerated his moody behavior and her feelings of insecurity that came from never knowing when he would come home. With great patience and gentleness, she finally suggested that he see a counselor.

The first counselor she called was not in but said at the end of the phone message, "God bless you, and call again." Ryan's wife had no idea before she called that the counselor was a Christian, but now she knew he was the one for her husband. Ryan reluctantly agreed to see the counselor, and after one-and-a-half years of regular visits, he broke through the strongholds of anger, bitterness and resentment.

By *receiving God's grace,* Ryan was able to overcome the pit-falls of perfectionism, obsession and controlling behavior. He was also able to free himself from his father's hurtful expectations. Grace imbued him with the ability to separate the person from the behavior and he no longer took it personally when his father expressed disappointment in him. He recognized that patience and acceptance, as well as forgiveness, are required to set us free from someone else's grip.

Ryan's father, however, has yet to break out of the cycle of insecurity and rejection he feels even from his own son. He needs to release Ryan and the lies about his own inadequacies. Through the grace that comes from Christ, he could do this and be transformed, made whole, secure and, most important, free.

Ryan is now living the life that God designed for him and his wife from the beginning. They still have problems, but with God's help they are able to work through them together. They live the abundant life that Jesus promised to everyone. They are free to enjoy each other and enjoy other people, even with all their faults (see Exod. 20).

God is able to do extraordinary things and provide them in excess—things that are beyond anything we can imagine or ask (see Eph. 3:20). At one time, life was not working for Ryan, but it is now.

Mary's Story

Life wasn't working for Mary either. She had prayed for years that God would help her in her dating relationships with men, but with no success. One thing Mary needed to do was change her attitude. She felt negative, angry and full of disillusionment and pessimism. She thought her life was never going to be any better; she was never going to find a man, be married or be happy.

Through Christian counseling, Mary discovered that she had never dealt with her feelings about her father. She felt that her father had rejected her and that he was disappointed she wasn't a boy. She had never grown close to her father emotionally. In fact, they seemed miles apart. Mary began to see a correlation between not getting emotionally close to the men she dated and not being emotionally close to her father. What could she do about that?

Mary wanted to be healed of her past. Because she was so hurt by the rejection she felt from her father, she discovered what she could do through Jesus that she was not able to do through self: forgive her father, forgive herself and forgive the men she'd been involved with who hurt and disappointed her. That empowered Mary to extend to her father the same gift of grace that she had received from God.

Life began to work for Mary. Her attitude became more positive and hopeful. It was easier for her to draw closer emotionally to the man she was currently dating. She was free to emotionally give of herself as well as receive. Within a few months, Mary's boyfriend asked her to marry him. Their love relationship continued to grow, and a few months later they married.

Not only was life working for Mary in her relationship with her husband, but it was also working with her father. She was able to reach out to her father and share with him how he hurt her emotionally and how rejected she felt by him. Her father apologized and indicated how sorry he was. This meant the world to Mary! She was so thankful for the grace of God to forgive her father and the courage to reach out to him. They started to develop a meaningful relationship and both were able to praise God and thank Him for the grace that saved them and their relationship.

What happened to both Ryan and Mary is healing grace in action. Their stories illustrate what it means to take the grace that God has given you and offer it to another. This is how hurting people become whole and how hurting relationships get mended.

No Longer a Victim

Now make the jump from what happened in their lives to what's happening in yours. Some of you are victims of your own bad choices and you are having a hard time admitting it. Give that thought a chance. Put this book down and pray about it right now and return to reading when you can agree that some faulty choices or faulty thinking on your part may actually be contributing to your pain. (We will talk about taking responsibility for our own attitudes and actions in the coming chapters.)

Not all people are victims of their own choices. Some are clearly victims of the abuses and errors or sins of others, particularly of those close to them. If that is your story, please know that healing grace is available to everyone, even to your offender.

Whether your problem is anger, fear, inadequacy, addiction to drugs or pornography, the message you need to hear is that you, too, can go forward to receive the abundant life God has for you. God's healing grace is sufficient for your cure (see 2 Cor. 12:9). Some people need to make major changes in how they think about themselves and the Lord's love for them. Others just need to receive His gift of grace. But no one has to remain a victim.

Healing grace enables us to move away from being victims of others' actions to being conquerors in Christ. By the power of the Holy Spirit and the transforming work of God's Word, we can get out of patterns of negative self-talk and into a mindset based on grace. We can let go of self-hatred and learn how to love and forgive ourselves and others because Christ unconditionally loves us.

We can break free from blaming others for our issues and from the bondage of unforgiveness. It is not God's will for you to wallow in resentment any longer.

When you receive the underserved favor of the Most High God, you will experience healing in your soul! No longer will that place of brokenness in your life be a crack in which bitter roots grow, but a spring from which grace can flow to others. Like Ryan and Mary, and others you have yet to read about, you will be able to enjoy freedom from feelings that may have bound you for years, and extend the favor of unmerited forgiveness to those who have hurt you.

The Author of Healing Grace

"Healing Grace" isn't simply a magical phrase or philosophy that we subscribe to as another self-help tool. And we (Norm and Larry) are not the authors of the ultimate healing grace. We hope this book will help you seek out that Author. He is Christ, and the grace He gives is eternal.

The premise to *healing grace* is that Jesus Christ has to rule in a person's heart in order for true healing to take place. The next chapter will outline the consequences of the life lived when self rules rather than Christ. When Christ is the center of your life, grace freely flows from Him to you and through Christ in you to others. He becomes for you the source of living water and the bread of life. Jesus becomes the center of your universe. The problems you have become smaller, easier to solve, and less of a threat to your existence and your personal worth when processed through Him.

Jesus says, "Follow Me. I Am. I Will. Fear Not. Just Believe" (see Matt. 4:19; 16:24; 19:21; John 10:27; Isa. 41:10; 46:9; 55:11; Josh. 1:9) and "You Can!" (see Mark 9:23). The results of letting Jesus be in charge of your life are amazing.

There was a man in the seventeenth century who discovered a fascinating principle. Dutch mathematician, astronomer and physicist Christiaan Huygens invented the pendulum clock and began manufacturing them to sell. One evening he was lying in bed and noticed that all of the pendulums were swinging in unison even though he knew for sure they hadn't started out that way. So he got out of bed and restarted them, purposefully setting them at different times to break the synchronized rhythm. In a brief period of time they began swinging together again. Years later scientists discovered that the largest clock with the strongest rhythm pulled the other pendulums into sync with itself. The strongest biological oscillator in our body is our heart and it acts like the clocks. It has the ability to pull every other bodily system into its own rhythm. When your heart is at peace, as ruled by Christ, all the rest of your body experiences the influence of His presence. But if self is at the center, your life is out of sync.

Spiritually speaking, when Jesus is at the center of your life or heart, His presence, His peace, is communicated to every aspect of your life, such as your body, your mind and your relationships. When Jesus is at the center, you will be amazed at the difference![5] And when Jesus is at the center of your life, what you do and say will reflect His grace, which we define as God's gift of unconditional love and forgiveness to us through Jesus Christ. Your grace-filled life will be one that is healed and is helping others heal through the gift of that grace. Stay with us, because the best is yet to come, and the best is what God is going to do in your life through His healing grace.

Pray the prayer below as we begin this journey together:

GOD,
Help me. I'm lost. I'm hungry. I'm hurting.
So many have hurt me.
My spouse, my parents, even my children.
I know that I must forgive in order to be forgiven.
I know that I must give grace in order to receive grace.
Teach me, Lord, how to do what I must.
Give me strength, Lord, to do it.
Teach me, Lord, to trust You.

CHAPTER 3

Who Is on the Throne of Your Life?

Saddam Hussein is considered one of the most ruthless leaders in the history of the world. He's right up there with Ramses, Nebuchadnezzar, Nero, Alexander, Stalin, Mussolini, Hitler, Pol Pot and Idi Amin. He tried his best to eliminate the people of Northern Iraq—the Kurds—by using nerve gas. When the issue of weapons of mass destruction led to confrontation with the United Nations and the United States, he chose almost passive indifference rather than acquiescence.

He claimed that a military confrontation with him would result in the "mother of all battles." He backed up defiant words with acts of cowardice by placing children in buildings that he knew the coalition would attack, and then tried to gain the emotional support of the world as he showed pictures of the innocent dead. He and his sons would take women captive, kill their husbands, rape the women and also kill them. If a person was even suspected of being an enemy, the outcome would be his torture and death.

Mass graves were commonplace in Iraq. Many families who lost loved ones still don't know where their final resting place is. Saddam and his sons bilked the country out of billions of dollars of oil money. When engaged by coalition forces, they allowed an inadequately armed force to be annihilated and oil wells to be destroyed in order to slow down the assault.

After a long, arduous search, Saddam was found in a hole in the ground where he lived like a rodent, hiding and afraid. After incarceration, he had the audacity to challenge his conditions and verbally abuse the judge presiding over his case. The outcome of his trial resulted in his death by hanging. Perhaps his death counts as some kind of atonement for the atrocities he committed. Saddam was a sociopath, and his end was the result of a life given to only one thing: SELF.

Sometime in the '60s it became quite attractive to put self in the forefront of every publication, every communication and every economic or political decision; our world became consumer driven. What do we hear on TV today? "You deserve it. Why wait? Indulge yourself now."

There is even a women's magazine called *Self*. It may be a good publication, but its title shows the idea of self being so important that people would create a publication to satisfy the desire for self-interest.

What if there were a periodical called *Others*? Do you think it would sell? Probably not. Frankly, our world is not interested, at least in large part, in helping others. Most people are looking out only for self. It's an indictment of our culture that we are so self-centered that we have a preoccupation with meeting our own "needs" rather than letting God meet our needs according to His riches in glory through Jesus Christ.

Your response to the above may be, "It's only natural that the human species, like other animals, will seek its own self-interest. After all it's the survival of the fittest, right?"

Wrong!

Getting back to the example of Saddam Hussein, he had what most people would describe as "having it all." After all, he had unlimited power, vast riches, huge palaces, cars, planes, yachts and pleasure from numerous sources. What else could he want? And yet, "what profit is it to a man if he gains the whole world, and loses his own soul?" (Matt. 16:26, *NKJV*).

Jesus has something more to say about this self-centeredness:

A young man walked up to Jesus one day and said, "Teacher, what good thing shall I do that I may obtain eternal life?"

And He said to him, "Why are you asking Me about what is good? There is only One who is good; but if you wish to enter into life, keep the commandments."

He asked Him, "Which ones?"

And Jesus said, "You shall not commit murder; you shall not commit adultery; you shall not steal; you shall not bear false witness; honor your father and mother; and you shall love your neighbor as yourself."

The young man said to Him, "All these things I have kept; what am I still lacking?"

Jesus said to him, "If you wish to be complete, go and sell your possessions and give to the poor, and you shall have treasure in heaven; and come, follow Me."

But when the young man heard this statement, he went away grieved; for he was one who owned much property (Matt. 19:16-22).

Did you ever wonder why this young man asked Jesus about what he needed to do to receive eternal life? Perhaps it was because he recognized that Jesus was the Christ, or that He was different from the phony religious leaders of the day. One thing is certain: that young man was dissatisfied with his life and knew there had to be something better for him. The riches that Saddam had did not satisfy any more than the riches of the young ruler who spoke to Jesus.

Jesus also knew that the young man had a thirst, and He challenged him. Jesus knew that the young ruler knew the commandments well. Notice that Jesus did not include all the Ten Commandments, and He also included a commandment not in the original ten: "love your neighbor as yourself." It is beyond the scope of this book to dissect the whole meaning of this interaction, but suffice it to say that the commandments Jesus mentioned were those that involved dealing with other people.

The rich young man knew there had to be something else, which is implied in the statement he made: "All these things I have kept; what am I still lacking?" There was a hunger deep inside of him; what he had been doing with his life was not working. Self was not getting it done the way he had hoped. He knew it, and he knew that Jesus knew it, hence his next question—a question that plagues many of us: "What am I still lacking?"

It wasn't as if he had almost everything he needed and he just had to add this final ingredient to the stew to make it right for consumption. He actually had missed the entire boat, the *grace* that was waiting to set him free—the grace that would make an eternal difference in his life.

Jesus said to him, "If you wish to be complete, go and sell your possessions and give to the poor, and you shall have treasure in heaven; and come, follow Me."

Jesus, in essence, was pointing out to him that it was not by external deeds that a man is justified before God, but by a heart full of the grace of God through a relationship with Christ and, in turn, relationships with others. This man's heart longed for the riches of the world, not for Christ. Jesus made it very clear that "where your treasure is, there will your heart be also" (Matt. 6:21). This man's treasure was in his possessions and not in his relationship with the Son of God, Jesus Christ. The rich young ruler declared by his actions that the comfort of riches was more important than the peace, joy and assurance of life that would have been his by making Christ the center of his life.

Who Comes First in Your Marriage?

Let's examine a couple, Jeremy and Angela. The main problem, at least on the surface, was Jeremy's problem with drugs and sexual addiction. It's not uncommon for both addictions to manifest together.

The real problem is that many men, who for the most part appear strong on the outside, are often weaker emotionally on the inside. On the whole, men have a more difficult time dealing with emotions stemming from rejection, verbal and physical abuse, anger, bitterness and resentment. Men tend to internalize (and stuff down) those emotions, leading to their intensification. Often they escape dealing with their emotions and problems through drugs, sex, gambling and even sports in excess.

On the other hand, women generally have a much easier time communicating and processing their emotions. Women, on the whole, can verbally deal with their problems and talk more easily with other women or seek counseling. Some may appear weaker on the outside, but they are usually stronger emotionally on the inside.

Jeremy and Angela are good examples of this description of external/internal strengths and weaknesses. When Angela found out that her husband, Jeremy, was involved with drugs and pornography, she wanted to divorce him. Jeremy responded in a positive way to her confrontation and was willing to change rather than be divorced from his wife. He sought counseling. Her initial reaction to his double addiction was predictable. She gave little to no support to him.

Perhaps some of you reading this book think that Jeremy doesn't deserve a second chance. Some might say it's all his fault. He'll never change. He deserves to be divorced. Perhaps that is what he deserves. But consider for a moment another option: *healing grace.*

Everyone is imperfect and falls short of God's perfect standard. Why do we so often expect to live with a perfect person (see Rom. 3:23)? We must acknowledge that our own faulty thinking is at least partially responsible for our own hurt. That being the case, how can we judge others—particularly our spouse—if they handle their insecurities incorrectly?

Jesus says, "If you have something in both your eyes that is so debilitating, so irritating that you cannot see, how can you possibly perform surgery on someone else's eye?" (see Matt. 7:1-7). In other words, if you have insecurities, faults, rejections, inadequacies, sin and disobedience to God, how can you possibly point the finger at another (spouse, friend, family member, co-worker, neighbor)?

Not that we have to be perfect before we can address sin or negative behavior in someone else's life, but that we must take care to examine ourselves, knowing that we're not above reproach. We must seek to speak to others with an attitude of grace rather than condemnation. It can be very hard when someone so close to you has so deeply wounded you, but following the example of Jesus and approaching that person with a heart of humility is a better way.

This is where Angela made a mistake after discovering Jeremy's involvement in drugs and pornography. At first she was willing to give him a second chance because of the children, but her anger, bitterness and resentment toward him led to some excessive self-centered reactions. One way she knew that she could really hurt him was to cut him off from any sexual activity.

Is this grace?

Most men would see this as punishment and judgment. Jesus said in the last Scripture reference, "Do not judge lest you be judged yourselves." Even if this couple did recover from this issue, what are the chances that some other problem might come up in the future? What if Angela is part of the problem? Will she expect Jeremy to treat her the same way she treated him? Too often it becomes a vicious cycle and no one wins in the end.

If this cycle were to continue, would their relationship have any chance of progressing into a healthy marriage? Only if they both were willing to give up self and let Christ be in charge of their lives as well as their marriage. Only through Jesus Christ could Jeremy and Angela really forgive each other. Only He could help them build a bridge of grace between them that would enable them to rebuild their relationship. Only with Him at the center could they learn to encourage and love each other, renew their intimacy and improve their communication.

They needed to tell each other the healing phrases, "I was wrong," "You were right," "I am sorry," "I forgive you," "Please forgive me" and "I love you." Learning to resolve problems brings healing to an individual as well as to his or her relationships. Working on problems together can actually draw you closer to one another and increase your love and intimacy.

In this case, who was putting self on the throne of his or her heart? Both Jeremy and Angela were to blame. Jeremy was dishonoring his wife. He was obtaining gratification through drugs and pornography in a way that really hurt her. Jeremy put himself and his perverted pleasure above the needs and interests of his wife and above his need for Christ.

Angela took the position of the irreconcilable spouse and became a martyr. She felt that she had suffered so much and had been wronged so terribly by her husband that she couldn't let him off the hook. Yet, for the sake of the children, she concluded, she would do the right thing, keep a stiff upper lip, sacrifice her own wants and needs and stay in the marriage. This stance only heightened her anger toward her husband. It did not bring healing to her or her marriage. It resulted in even more anger, which contributed to an unhealthy atmosphere for the children.

Angela allowed herself to hold tightly to her feelings of anger, bitterness and resentment, refusing to accept Jeremy's attempts at reconciliation. She allowed the breach in their relationship to become a huge gaping hole with little chance of repair.

No relationship can sustain that kind of self-centeredness. When self is in charge, only what *I* want matters. Occasionally *I* will give something nominal to *you* so that *I* can manipulate *you* into giving *me* what *I* want. Eventually *I* take up so much space that there is no longer even the slightest room for Jesus or anyone else.

In order to make you truly aware of this process, take a look at a more academic approach as outlined in the diagram labeled "The Defeated Christian" at the end of this chapter. This diagram represents you. It is made up of spirit, soul, body and relationships, with self in the center. It's as if self says, "Thank You, Jesus, for saving me, but I've got to be me; so, Jesus, You stay in my self-made closet. If I need You, I'll let You out of the closet to help me again, just as I let You save me." Unfortunately, this is what so many Christians do consciously or unconsciously.[1]

When Self Short-Circuits

How do you know who is in the center of your life or on the throne of your heart? Ask yourself how you handle the frustrations of life. If through self, then the outcome is anger, bitterness, resentment, and other negative emotions. Of course this will hurt your relationship with your spouse, children, friends, and others. This also will hurt your soul (your mind, emotions, will—your personality). This in turn tends to adversely affect your self-esteem and make you feel insecure and inadequate. Then comes guilt due to all the anger. Or perhaps self stuffs or represses anger, which in turn brings on depression. Although a person may have a genetic predisposition to depression, anger and unforgiveness greatly exacerbate it.

What follows is that you begin to worry all the more (see Phil. 4:6-7), giving in to doubts and fears (see 2 Tim. 1:7) about life and what is going to happen to you, your marriage, your family and other important relationships. This then creates more stress and anxiety. Emotionally, self is really hurting, as are many of your relationships. Next, self seeks to escape all of this (something we'll address in depth later) by fantasizing, abusing alcohol or other drugs, gambling, eating, and/or seeking out inappropriate sexual pleasure or other diversions. When any one of these becomes an obsession, it becomes an addiction. When this happens, even self begins to lose control and the addiction begins to take over. (Do you see any of these things in yourself?)

A troubled soul often brings about a hurting body with many physical symptoms. The more we allow damaging emotions to exist and grow in our life, the more we place our physical body at risk. There is a link between being self-centered and building emotional turmoil and eventually having our body keep score in the form of numerous ailments, such as heart and vascular problems, gastrointestinal problems, headaches, skin conditions, genitourinary tract disorders, pain and inflammation, lung and breathing problems, and immune impairment.[2]

In his book *Deadly Emotions*, Dr. Don Colbert said, "Without a doubt, hostility, rage and anger are at the top of the list of toxic emotions that generate an extreme stress reaction."[3] And if you stuff your emotions, the more powerful the explosion will be when they can't be contained any longer. When you experience negative emotions, for whatever reason, it is far better to express them to God than attempt to stuff them. Job expressed everything from confusion to pain to anger, and in the book of Psalms, David wrote repeatedly of the wide range of emotions he was experiencing.

Other emotions as well take their toll on the body. There is a well-documented link between depression and disease, including a much higher risk of heart attacks.[4] Guilt and shame not only eat away at the body but they also lead to an endless loop of negative thinking. Fear is associated with a wide variety of diseases and in extreme cases can lead to sudden death. Take the time to read a biblical account of this in 1 Samuel 25.

When we are ruled by self, it's so easy to fall into jealousy and envy. These are all-consuming emotions that will eat away at you and taint all that you experience. Jealousy is a partner with resentment, and it's toxic. Scripture says:

A sound heart is life to the body, but envy is rottenness to the bones (Prov. 14:3, *NKJV*).

For wrath kills a foolish man, and envy slays a simple one (Job 5:2, *NKJV*).

Now the works of the flesh are evident which [include] . . . envy (Gal. 5:19,21, *NKJV*).

When we harbor these attitudes, self begins to short-circuit. At this point, self is not doing a very good job, is it? So what, then, is the answer? What do you do? Are you tired of self being in control and trying to do it all?

There *is* an answer. You don't have to live a defeated Christian life or have a miserable marriage or family life. Rather you can live a meaningful life through Jesus Christ. A living, breathing relationship with Him—the One who died to heal your brokenness—is where healing grace begins.

There is hope, as you will appreciate from Pam's example. Pam was a widow for several years. Her husband died in a car accident. She was angry at God for letting her husband die; she was angry at the doctors for not being able to save him; she was angry at her husband for dying; and she was angry at herself for not doing better through it all.

Her husband's death devastated her so much that she shut down and withdrew from life except to go to church and to the grocery store. She was becoming an agoraphobic (someone who fears leaving the confines of a safe environment like the house). Fortunately, she had two sensitive Christian friends who were concerned about her and brought her in for counseling. They took turns bringing her 100 miles for each session until she was able to drive herself.

Pam gradually overcame the agoraphobia as well as the depression and anxiety. How was she able to do this? Through self?

No.

Only as Pam was willing to give up self to be crucified with Jesus was she able through Christ to live out her faith and experience healing grace. Through Jesus (see diagram II, "The Victorious Christian"), Pam developed the attitude of Christ. Rather than living in defeat, she was able to become victorious over her grief. She began to experience a more meaningful life and to exhibit the fruit of the Spirit: love, joy, peace, patience, kindness, goodness, faithfulness, gentleness and self-control. Through Jesus, she had the strength to do what she had not been able to do through self.

She discovered how God's grace is sufficient and how His strength was made perfect in her weakness. Pam recognized that her faith had become dormant. As she actualized her faith through Jesus, her needs were met according to God's riches in glory through Christ. Her peace and joy were restored as she trusted Christ. The hope she experienced through the power of the Holy Spirit lifted her out of depression, despair, fear and anxiety (see Gal. 2:20; 5:22-23; 1 Cor. 15:57; John 10:10; Phil. 4:13,19; 2 Cor. 12:9; Rom. 15:13).

As Jesus became Lord of her life, Pam was able to appropriate the same grace that saved her, enabling her to forgive the doctors, her husband and even herself. This was a major breakthrough for Pam as she had some very negative thoughts. She again put to work her faith in Christ as God's grace healed her of guilt and self-condemnation.

Pam, for the first time, understood and applied 1 John 4:9 to her life. She thanked God that through Jesus Christ she could:

1. Live the victorious Christian life (see 1 Cor. 15:57)
2. Be more than a conqueror in life (see Rom. 8:37)
3. Have more abundant life (see John 10:10)
4. Enjoy everlasting life (see John 3:16; 17:3)

In Christ, you too can experience and live out these four truths. As John 8:32 tells us, we shall know the truth and the truth will set us free.

The Irony of Escapism

When controlled by self, false roads to freedom seduce us into booby traps set by the devil himself. Once we get stuck in one or more of these traps—or addictions—we are in bondage. As mentioned earlier, when struggling with pressure, pain and problems, the world (and self) entices us to escape via fantasy, drug and/or alcohol abuse, gambling, overeating, and engaging in pornography or other perverted sexual behaviors. Even seemingly good things, such as watching TV, cleaning the house, working long hours and playing sports can become unhealthy escapes when done excessively.

If you are old enough, you will remember the actor Steve McQueen in the signature role of Captain Virgil "The Cooler King" Hilts in *The Great Escape* (1963). It was based on a true story of men held in a high-security prison camp in Nazi Germany during World War II. The soldiers were placed there because of their intelligence and propensity for escape. Undaunted by the level of difficulty in this "escape-proof" camp, the prisoners dug a tunnel and left the enemy camp in large groups. These allied prisoners joined together in a sophisticated, collaborative effort to free themselves from their cruel tormenters.

Why did they go to such lengths to be free? The desire for freedom is almost universal. People will go through any number of difficulties—even risk the ultimate sacrifice of death—to escape from captivity. Like the men in that story, apart from Christ, all of humanity is enslaved to sin and thus "captured" by the enemy (see 2 Tim. 2:26; Titus 3:3; 2 Pet. 2:19). Likewise, men and women subconsciously submit to the slavery of dead works or rules of religion that keep them captive. Even while in bondage, however, there is still a desire within them to find freedom from those things. Why do you suppose this is?

The obvious answer is that no man or animal wishes to be locked up, bound or under someone else's control. We are created in such a way as to mimic our creator God. God is unparalleled in terms of the ability to control His (or anyone else's) circumstances. He can create a universe with a spoken word. He can bless or curse with the same word. Jesus had the power to heal the sick or cast out dark spiritual forces called demons with just a word. Again, He was the one who said that you could be free just by knowing His word: "And you shall know the truth and the truth shall set you free" (John 8:32).

If it's freedom that all men desire, then why do we so rarely seek the one who created us to be free—the one who lived, died and rose from the grave to keep us free? As you read this book, our hope is that you will desire more and more to seek your freedom in God instead of through the counterfeit escapes offered by the world. Some of you may say that you're not in any kind of physical or spiritual bondage. You do not believe that you have any cause to seek additional freedom beyond that which you already enjoy. But each of us at some point in our life will live in some kind of prison. If you've already found freedom in Christ, then let what you read here be a resource to you as you reach out to those still in bondage around you. Let's examine some common escapes and prisons they lead to.

A number of years ago, in a small town in the British Isles, it was claimed that a newly constructed jail had an escape-proof cell. Harry Houdini, the great escape artist known all over the world, was invited to test it to see if it really was escape-proof. He accepted the invitation, having once boasted that no jail could hold him.

Houdini entered the cell, and the jailer closed the door behind him. Houdini listened to the sound of the key being slipped into the lock. The jailer withdrew the key and left. Houdini took out his tools and started the process of working on that cell door. But it didn't work out the way he expected. Nothing seemed to work, and the hours passed. He was puzzled because he had never before failed to open a locked door.

Finally the great Houdini admitted defeat and leaned against the door in resigned exhaustion. It suddenly opened. The jailer had never locked it. The only place the door was locked was in Houdini's mind.

I've done it and so have you; we've locked ourselves in because of what we thought and believed. As a result, we lock ourselves away from the hope and faith that lead to blessing. Instead of enjoying the assurance and freedom that come from belonging to God, we become the negative people we imagine ourselves to be. Nathaniel Hawthorne captured this dilemma beautifully in *The House of Seven Gables*: "What other dungeon is so dark as one's own heart! What jailer so inexorable as one's self!"

What is ironic is that the ways in which we consciously or subconsciously seek to escape often open the doors to our very prison. Some of these prisons are the ones we have created ourselves; others have created for us; and still others Satan has created. Yes, Satan exists. The Bible says that he was the lead angel who led the worship of God. But it wasn't enough—he coveted more power. He tried to put himself above God. It didn't work and God threw him out of heaven. Many other angels fell into the same trap. In fact, one-third of all the angels in heaven were cast out along with Satan because they chose to rebel and follow him instead of God (see Isa. 14:12-15).

Satan is our enemy. But he can only *suggest* a course of action leading to destruction; he cannot make us *do* anything. We, unfortunately, choose a wrong course of action when we heed his suggestions and try to do it our way.

So let's move out of the theological realm and into the practical. What are some of the prisons of our own creation? How do we escape those circumstances in a *healthy* way? You may have your own particular circumstance that you feel is your hell or prison. Perhaps it's something like the examples of the very difficult personal circumstances given earlier in this chapter.

What causes a spouse to seek greener pastures? Is it the allure of better sex? Is it the possibility of getting into a better situation? More security? More significance? Fewer problems? The motivations that move us to bad behavior are numerous, but consider that the payoff is rarely worth the consequences.

Ryan Revisited

Remember Ryan? He sought some release from a situation where he felt bracketed by marriage. When a cute, young blonde with a bubbly personality came along, Ryan responded emotionally as well as physically. Satan was whispering to him, "Hey, this woman is the real thing. What you married was a mistake. This is really what you want and what you need. Check it out. A little affection will never hurt anything. It's not as if you're having sex or something, and besides, you deserve some pleasure with all the problems you're having with your wife."

Problems? They weren't having any problems to speak of—the enemy took a weakness of testosterone-induced attraction, mixed it with the lie of marital problems and promised Ryan something better if he stepped beyond the borders of God's plan.

But guess what? Nothing better came of that relationship for Ryan. Although being in the arms of an attractive woman offered a temporary escape from his problems, it wasn't beneficial. It only added to the stress and destruction of his other un-dealt-with issues. The penalty to be paid was not worth the temporary pleasure of disobedience to God. And just when he thought God was neither watching nor present in his situation, God allowed Ryan the distinct displeasure of having to face up to his wife and look her in the eye and explain why he was not at work that day.

How did he get into such a situation? He allowed the unchecked lust in his life and his need for an escape from life's pressures to become justification for sin.

You may wonder why Ryan would give us permission to display his dirty laundry in this book. Soon you'll discover that being honest with yourself and your spouse sets you free. It gives you the courage and strength to escape from the prison you have created for yourself. When you're honest about yourself, you won't be threatened by the truth; you will be set free by it. You will be set free by Jesus, who is the way, the truth and the life (see John 14:6).

Here is what set Ryan up for failure: He had grown up in an alcoholic household in which he was trained to believe that his security (love) and significance (power to do good) were based on performance. If his performance was bad, he felt threatened and worthless. If his performance was good, he felt content and fulfilled. Our self-worth is not based on what we do but on who we really are. It is based on what God has been willing to do for us—ransoming our lives through Jesus' death and resurrection. For God loved the world so much that He gave up His only Son so that whoever believed in Him would not spend eternity in hell, but live forever in heaven (see John 3:16).

When Ryan was seeing another woman, his wife didn't beg him to stop or ask why he did what he did. She simply said, "Cease and desist or hit the pavement." She had enough self-respect (something Ryan never had because of a topsy-turvy childhood and a poor understanding of who he was) to realize she was worth more than that. She wasn't going to tolerate his behavior. She brought consequences to bear on the situation. She drew a line in the sand. She was not going to force him to stay with her against his will. She simply was not going to settle for a husband who was unfaithful.

God is a lot like that. He will not tolerate rebellion, because He deserves better. But God will not force us to do something against our will. He, like Ryan's wife, will continue to call us to have a change of mind and heart about our rebellious ways until we die. If we do not learn, change and grow by accepting the grace He freely offers us through Christ, He will cry for us until we reach the point where we are permanently separated from Him. When speaking of separation in marriage, the law calls this divorce. When speaking of eternity separated from His grace and presence, God calls it hell.

You may be saying, "Well, what about my no-good spouse? He (she) is just like Ryan." Well, yes and no. Ryan chose to turn around and do the correct thing. Your spouse may or may not do that. Some people may not wake up and realize they've been living and believing a lie. Or they may be so miserable in their life that it does not matter to them.

What does matter is what *you* do—how you respond. Are you going to whip out a carton of ice cream and a bottle of booze and eat and drink yourself into a deeper pit, or are you going to seek help from someone who has the wisdom and compassion to truly make a difference in your life? Are you going to surrender to the truth about God's love and grace?

We need to understand that when we want to get out of a hole, we need to stop digging deeper. When you've had a one-night stand because you were depressed about your wife leaving you, you don't need to continue seeking out liaisons that might give you HIV. When you went off the wagon because your mother died, you don't need to sell everything you have so that you can drink yourself into a prolonged stupor. If what you're doing isn't working, why keep doing it? There's a better way.

We all have times when we wish to escape. That's normal. Some situations can leave us extremely depressed, hopeless and helpless, feeling angry, bitter, resentful, frustrated, tearful and left without respect for ourselves or others. You may even hate yourself because of wrong decisions. But stop digging a deeper hole! The new prison you create will be far worse than the climb to get out of your original pit of emotional pain. Jesus is ready not only to extend a hand to you but also to jump right in with you and push you up and out of your pit. Will you make room for Him to do that?

Mario's Story

Mario struggles with bipolar disorder and has spent time in prison for grand theft auto, drug dealing and drug usage. He is depressed. He also has diabetes, and when his blood sugar is out of control, his depression worsens. He has four children: One is autistic and one has attention deficit hyperactivity disorder (ADHD). The most important thing in his life aside from his young daughter is his wife. She's a stable woman, and the only stable force in his life.

Mario grew up in the barrio in Amarillo with a family of one brother, two half-brothers and one half-sister. His mother became a lesbian and was in a short-term relationship with another woman. As one of the oldest children, and because of the substance abuse problems of his parents, Mario had to raise his younger brothers and sisters. Eventually his mother's lesbian partner died of drug abuse and Mario's mother remained physically and verbally abusive. His father was nowhere to be found.

This "father" left home when Mario was 15. Mario started dealing drugs at age 17 and used them on and off for most of his life. Alcohol and drugs were his escape from the perverted and abusive experiences of his youth. He became a fighter in response to frequent harassment he encountered on the streets. Do you ever wonder why people make choices like that? Do you think one day they just wake up and decide, "Hey, I'm going to leave home so I can experience this great life living in an alley, smoking weed, stealing and selling cocaine to anyone with money." Obviously not. It's a progression of wrong choices that lead people into that lifestyle.

People engage in escapism for obvious reasons. They're in a prison they can no longer endure mentally, emotionally or physically—or at least they think they can't. And it's true! Without help they can't endure, nor can you or I.

Let's look at Mario again. He lived with abusive, self-centered and deviant parents who had made choices for their own gratification without any real appreciation for what it would do to their kids. When parents act without regard for the needs of their children, they set them up for social disaster. Perhaps this was just a repetition of what they themselves had experienced as children. Perhaps Mario's mother was tired of being abused by men and decided in a bizarre, rebellious way to engage in a same-sex relationship. Whatever the motivation, the results were devastating for her children.

Mario responded by escaping into drugs and alcohol. He learned through observation that the best way to gain material possessions was to sell drugs. It was easy, requiring nothing more than a street education and some muscle. He had all of that. What he did not realize, though, was that by becoming a client of his own product he could not sell enough drugs to keep himself adequately supplied to meet his addiction. Stealing cars was the next step. Again, it was easy to do, and with the connections he had established in prison, there were plenty of fences who could help sell his stuff.

That's when God intervened in a most unusual fashion. Mario was driving east on I-40 when he picked up a hitchhiker in the rain. He was an unusual fellow—older and with a quiet demeanor. He said he just needed a ride to the next truck stop. The man asked Mario about his life. Mario told him. The hitchhiker didn't say anything. He didn't condemn Mario; he just had a look of sadness in his eyes at what he'd heard. When they got to the truck stop, he bought Mario a cup of coffee and spoke of God. They left the truck stop together walking side by side. When Mario turned to speak to the man, he was gone. There was no trace of him. He was just gone.

At the time, Mario didn't realize what had happened. He was in a state of shock. However, this was the day when he realized he needed to change his life and stop doing drugs. He started going to Narcotics Anonymous where he met his sponsor and gave his life to Christ. As he reflects on his story, he realizes that God sent an angel to communicate His truth and to provide healing grace to his life.

The story doesn't end there, and it's no Cinderella story either. The truth is, Mario sought escape via a new addiction: work. He went from doing drugs to working a full-time job renting houses. He was also a bounty hunter. Whatever way he could make a legitimate dollar he did it. Although his work was all legal, it still led to another form of destruction. He said he was doing it for his family and for his friends. Just as he had developed a savior mentality taking care of his siblings while growing up, so too he started doing the same things for his friends. He had his group of homies. He called them "my men"—guys he was trying to help out of their particular prisons of drug and alcohol abuse.

Despite his attempts at being "good," Mario had a relapse. He went back on drugs. After an argument with his wife, he tried to commit suicide by driving his truck into a tree. Now even his wife was ready to give up on him.

The point here again is that there is no escape from problems in this life, there is only strength to deal with them. Our enemy the devil walks around like a roaring lion seeking someone to devour. Satan doesn't just lead us into temptation to do stupid stuff. He seeks to find someone to rip to shreds for the purpose of inflicting pain because his only motivation is pure hatred.

Although this was a very low point in Mario's life, he found himself in a teachable moment. Someone advised him to write down on a sheet of paper everything he felt God actually wanted for His life (e.g., stability, success, joy, freedom from drugs, freedom from depression, and good health). Instead of focusing on the lies of the enemy, they encouraged him to spend one hour a day focusing on the truth of God's Word.

Jesus said that the truth will set us free. Training the mind by meditating on God's Word is one of the keys to successful living. One of Joyce Meyer's favorite sayings when attacking wrong thinking is to call it "stinking thinking."[5] The admonition in the Bible is, "don't copy the behavior and customs of this world, but be a new and different person with a fresh newness in all you do and think. Then you will learn from your own experience how his ways will really satisfy you" (Rom. 12:2, *TLB*).

Mario began to spend significant time in the Word of God, receiving and believing truth. As a result of speaking his affirmations about the kind of man God wanted him to be, his mind began to change. Once his mind changed, his behavior changed. Within a couple weeks people started noticing a difference. They began to see Mario's peace and stability reflected in his life. His kids even noticed a difference. Eventually he and his wife reconciled their differences and he began to love her as God desires for all men to love their wives.

Take a Look at Yourself

Now think about your own situation. What's going on in your life? Are you controlled and dominated by fear, anger and resentment? Are you having an affair or dealing with someone who is? Are you a successful professional who's doing cocaine on the weekends at high-brow parties? Or are you a six-pack-a-day blue-collar worker? Do you work 80 hours a week to provide for your insecurity, or rather, as you would put it, your family? Do you lose yourself in the fantasies of pornography to find some excitement in life? After achieving all you have in life, is your self-esteem still nonexistent and your heart still empty?

Some may have other great escapes like food, gambling, shopping or sitting in front of a television, living vicariously through the actors on the screen while avoiding the very people in their home. The reason we attempt to escape at all is to change how we feel, to try to make ourselves feel better and to somehow numb the miserable feelings that gnaw at us from within. These escapes do numb us, so much so that they paralyze us from dealing with our misery and from walking through the true healing process.

Those of you who have spent any time incarcerated or have recovered from any type of addiction—pornography, alcohol, drugs, nicotine, food, sex, and so forth—can probably testify that your addiction-free (prison-free) days have been the most satisfying of your life. It may have been difficult for you to break free. It may still be difficult. But doesn't the freedom you've experienced make it worth the sweat and tears?

Remember Houdini? How did he get free? How do you get free from your addiction? What is the *real* escape? We will get to this in the chapters to come. Please trust that in due time, the secret of release from bondage will become understandable to you. Whether you have been the victim or the initiator of destruction, you will be able to find release from your personal prison through the healing power of God's grace. Look forward to what's ahead—to becoming all you were created to be as you trust the One who created you and allow Him to set you *free*.

DIAGRAM I

Defeated Christian

Spirit
Saved but:
Self still in charge of my life
(Luke 6:46; 1 John 1:19;
Ephesians 2:8)

Relationships
1. Dissension; strife, conflict, quarrel
2. Separation
3. Divorce
4. Dysfunctional families
5. Violence/hurtful interactions
   a. murder
   b. rape
   c. physical, emotional, verbal, sexual abuse

Self
In the Center—"My Way,"
Not Jesus' Way

Soul (personality)
Frustrations of life through self
result in anger, resentment and
hostility, which give foothold to
devil (Ephesians 4:26-32)

Body
Numerous physical symptoms:
1. Tension headaches
2. Colitis/spastic colon
3. Stomach problems
4. Skin problems
5. Heart palpitations
6. Respiratory ailments
7. Fatigue
8. Others

Self-esteem
Low
Insecurity
Inadequacy
Inferiority
Guilt

Will
My way

Mental
(Can become addictions)
Escape through:
Drugs
Sex
Food
Work
Money
Gambling

Emotions
Confused
Hurting
Depressed
Anxious
Fear
Worry
Doubts

DIAGRAM II

Victorious Christian

Spirit

- Born again (John 3:3-16; Acts 2:38-39; Romans 8:9-11)
- New creature in Christ (2 Corinthians 5:17)
- Crucified with Christ (Galations 2:20)
- Living through Christ (John 4:9)
  a. victorious life (1 Corinthians 15:57)
  b. more-than-conquerers life (Romans 8:37)
  c. more abundant life (John 10:10)
  d. eternal life (John 3:16; 17:13)
  e. fruitful life (Galations 5:16-23)
     i. peace (Philippians 4:6-7)
     ii. joy (John 15:5-12)

Relationships

1. Reconciled to one another by grace (2 Corinthians 5:18-20; 2 Peter 3:18; Hebrews 4:16)
2. Love one another (1 John 4:7-8; 1 Corithians 13)
3. Trust (Proverbs 3:5-6; Psalm 32:10b)
4. Respect (1 Peter 2:17; 3:7; 1 Timothy 3:2-5)
5. Helpful communication (Ephesians 4:29)
6. Forgiving each other (Ephesians 4:32)
7. Praying for each other (James 5:13-15)
8. Worship (Matthew 18:20)

JESUS CHRIST
Is Lord! Not Self
(Galatians 2:20; John 1:14)

Soul (personality)

1. Mind/attitude of Christ— Christlike behavior (Philippians 2:5)
2. Strength through Christ (Philippians 4:13; Ephesians 6:10)
3. Needs met through Christ (Philippians 4:19)
4. Will of God (1 Thessalonians 5:16-18)
5. Healthy self-esteem through Christ (Galatians 2:20)
6. Damaged emotions healed (2 Kings 20:5; 1 Peter 2:24; Psalm 147:3)

Body

Healing: Isaiah 53:4-5; Psalm 103:2-3; Matthew 8:1-3, 17; 1 Peter 2:24
1. Sin
2. Physical
3. Emotional
4. Mental
5. Spirital

CHAPTER 4

Are You Ready for Change?

When the movie *Alien* debuted many years ago, it captivated and terrified audiences, becoming one of the greats in the history of science fiction movies. The astronaut played by Sigourney Weaver found herself face to face with an ancient alien. Imagine the scariest, most hideous creature you've ever seen, a beast as big and brutal as a dragon released from the pit of hell. That was the Alien. It had two mouths, the inner one had teeth that resembled that of a skeleton's but extended several feet from its body so that it could devour its prey in one bite. It had a huge green, greasy head and a tail so long and fierce that it could whip its opponent's head off.

What was the astronaut's reaction to this beast?

The same reaction you and I would have: terror, fear, repulsion.

Imagine a person who had physical and emotional characteristics resembling those of the Alien.

How would *you* react to that person?

If you're honest, you would at least feel afraid, repulsed and possibly threatened or intimidated. Most of us would do a quick double-take and make for the nearest exit.

Let me tell you about a real person like this. Her name is Sarah. She was a 49-year-old Jewish woman referred to me (Larry) for counseling by the director of a convalescent nursing home. The director described Sarah to me as someone whom she had "no idea what to do for." Frankly, I didn't know what to do for her either when I first saw her.

The lights were off in her room, the blinds closed. Her physical appearance was ghastly. She had no eyelids, ears, lips, nose or hair. Her skin and physical features were replaced with a convoluted, leather-like hide.

I spoke to her, but she did not answer or look up. She didn't say one word during the entire session. For the second session I brought in a Christian psychiatrist who told me Sarah was impossible and beyond help. She continued in our sessions in desperate silence. Finally, at the end of the third session, I told her, "Sarah, I am not going to give up on you. Before I come back next week, I want you to touch one person with your life." I trusted the Lord to help her to do this.

Sarah had attempted suicide nine times. The ninth time she barely cheated death after setting her house on fire. Doctors said "she should have died." By God's grace she survived the attempt. However, like many of the wrong choices we make, there were some dramatic consequences for her. She had second- and third-degree burns over 90 percent of her body, from head to toe. She was grotesquely deformed. An initial encounter with her was nothing less than horribly shocking. It was like something out of a horror movie. She had spent months in the hospital before moving into the nursing home. Although she had physically recovered from her initial burns, she continued to suffer from a more deadly enemy than fire—emotions of anger, hopelessness and despair.

How could anyone be expected to help someone who so desperately wanted to end her life? She was so fragile, hurting and ugly, inside and out. I thought, *What problem in her life could be so horrible that she had attempted to give up on life nine times?* Shouldn't she be allowed to die? After all, she is of an age to make autonomous decisions. She has a free will. She has the capability to choose what she wants. Many would say, "Just allow her to do what is 'best' for her and for society. She has nothing to live for, nothing to gain."

What would you say?

Have you ever hated yourself and your life so much that you repeatedly attempted to kill yourself?

Do you have little or nothing to live for?

Do you think that God made a mistake when He made you?

Do you feel there is no hope for you?

Sarah may change your mind about a lot of things.

The Power of Giving

On the fourth session with Sarah, it was evident that something had changed. I opened the door of her room slowly, not knowing what to expect. Would I see a faceless woman sulking in her bed, awaiting her death, or would I find someone willing to fight for her life? For the first time in our limited interactions, she was sitting up in bed. The blinds were open and the light shone through with a warmth not previously felt in her room. To top it off, she was looking right at me.

"Sarah," I said with hope in my voice. "Something good has happened to you."

After two or three minutes of trying to articulate a response, she was able to say, "You know it has."

She explained how she had reached out to a man in a wheelchair and he had responded with an act of kindness in return. Acts of grace are the building blocks of relationships, and although Sarah did not know it, she was beginning to build bridges of grace that would change her life forever.

That she encountered someone who saw her in all her ugliness and yet did not reject her made the difference. She experienced a similar response from others as she made small steps out of her comfort zone to reach out to them. Soon she started participating in craft-making at the convalescent home, using her hands to create something of value instead of using them to destroy her life.

As weeks went by, she became known among all of the nursing home patients. She would make rounds on all nine floors, looking for people she could lovingly touch and in return receive grace in her life—something she had so desperately needed and sought without success before her physical trauma. It was as if she stepped out of her house for the first time and smelled the scent of a world she'd never known—one filled with the sweet aroma of lovely flowers planted by God in the garden of her heart.

After being severely neglected by her parents and four husbands, her life was finally taking a turn for good. She was beginning to love—and therefore really live—perhaps for the first time in her life. Sarah was ready for change, and change she did. She experienced grace—she gave it and received it.

Are you also ready for change?

Overcoming Fear

Maybe you're ready, but you're afraid. You've tried to change before. Failed marriages, failed diets, failed attempts at reconciliation and rehabilitation have left you weary, and wary of your own ability to truly follow through with real change.

Maybe you're worried about what others might think of you, or you're afraid of disappointing them. What if things don't go the way you (or they) expect? What if you relapse?

Sarah's son, who was a psychiatrist in another state, was one of these voices. He'd given up on his mother. He doubted what the grace of God could do to transform her.

About three months into Sarah's treatment, he called me and asked me not to help her. He felt that "not only was she beyond help," but also that "she was not worthy of help nor worthy to live." Obviously her son had some anger, bitterness and resentment of his own. It is heartbreaking to see that many of the problems experienced by people are passed down from generation to generation.

A few months later, things changed for the whole family. Sarah recovered and spent some time living with the director of nursing while she was in transition. When Sarah moved into her own apartment, I was invited to a Passover celebration with Sarah's whole family present. Her two daughters rejoiced in the transformation of their mother into a kind, gracious and loving person. In fact they were so impressed by the power of Christ's love to change her that they eventually came to accept Jesus as their Lord and Savior as well.

I will never forget what happened when her son opened the door for me. I did not know how he would respond, but he quickly alleviated my concerns when he embraced me for what seemed like minutes.

"I am so sorry for what I said to you about my mother. Would you please forgive me?" he said.

"Of course," I replied, having already forgiven him long ago.

"Thank you so much for not taking my advice. Thank you for helping Mom and not giving up on her. She is truly a changed woman beyond what any psychiatrist could ever dream of or hope for."

Fear is like a videotape that continually replays our most haunting experiences, embarrassing moments, rejections, failures, hurts and disappointments. Fear keeps you from acting on that "yes" to change. The message of the fear video is clear: Life is full of these experiences and they *will* repeat themselves. Fear causes us to say, "I can't do it. I may fail."

It's amazing that many people fear life itself. The fear of life is actually more debilitating than the fear of death. Fear disables. Fear shortens life. Fear cripples our relationships with others. Fear blocks our relationship with God. Fear makes life a chore. How strange it is for Christians to choose to imprison themselves in fear, especially when Christ came to set captives free. We have freedom in Christ, yet we often choose to walk through life in a morbid cell of fear, shut away from people and life's experiences.

Fear is a tool of Satan to cripple and control us. He wants us to live in the grip of fear. But this isn't God's way for us. "God did not give us a spirit that makes us afraid, but a spirit of power and love and self-control" (2 Tim. 1:7, *NCV*). There are literally hundreds of verses that deal with our fears, anxieties, insecurities, doubts, guilt and worry.

For example, the Word says to throw all your troubles on Jesus for He is the one who not only cares about you, but also He can actually make your situation better (see 1 Pet. 5:7).

God's grace is the answer to our problems—and our fears. What the Lord wants you to do now is to say yes to Him. Saying yes to believing and receiving the new life that He has for you will bring lasting changes—just as it did for Sarah. She was sick and tired of being sick and tired. She was ready for change.

She had nothing to lose in giving her life to Jesus, for she had totally given up on her life nine different times.

Jesus pleads with us to accept His grace. You do not have to continue to endure pain and suffering without the hope of healing. Life can be better. Let's look at what Jesus says for us to do and why:

"Come to Me, all who are weary and heavy-laden, and I will give you rest. Take My yoke upon you, and learn from Me, for I am gentle and humble in heart; and you shall find rest for your souls. For My yoke is easy, and My load is light" (Matt. 11:28-30).

In this verse Jesus does something that no other "religious" leader has ever done. He claims to have the power to relieve our burdens. He simply says, "Come to Me," not "Do this or do that and then you may find relief." He just says, "Come."

Are you weary?

Are you heavy-laden?

In other words, do you have emotional or spiritual baggage? Are you burdened by shame, anger or guilt over past failures that have set the tone for the rest of your existence?

Are you ready for change?

Jesus says, "Come to Me."

"I will give you rest," says the Good Shepherd. He will relieve you of every failure, every burden and every emotional scar you thought could never heal. He can and He wants to and He will. But you have to go to Him.

Ready for Change

Robert and Renae were ready for change. They wanted to get married, but they recognized they had some individual problems that negatively affected their relationship. They sought counseling individually and as a couple.

Robert had grown up in a dysfunctional family that was constantly fighting, arguing, yelling and hurting one another verbally, mentally, emotionally and sometimes even physically. Robert felt like he never did anything right. His parents always found fault with him. His father was especially cruel. Robert felt rejected. He felt like a loser, and so his attitude in general exhibited anger and defensiveness. If things didn't go his way, he'd respond in anger and attempt to blame it on someone else. He did this with Renae. Although Renae loved Robert, she wouldn't let him get away with projecting blame on her. She accepted that she was at fault at times, but not all the time.

Another issue that affected Robert and Renae's relationship was that Robert had a daughter out of wedlock. Renae had some concerns about Robert's relationship with his daughter's mother and how she would be able to handle this situation. She felt anxious and depressed, which affected her relationship with Robert in a negative way and eventually hindered her at work.

Although Robert and Renae had a saving relationship with Jesus, neither one really let Jesus be Lord of their life and their relationship. But they determined, with God's help, to change this. Robert didn't want to be selfish, angry and self-centered. Renae didn't want her emotions to get in the way anymore and she didn't want to fear dealing with Robert's anger. They recognized that their relationship was just not working, so they resolved to do something about it.

Robert began confronting his hurt and pain from his childhood. He recognized how this had created the anger in his life and how it was adversely affecting his life and relationships now. He realized that he needed to forgive his father and mother and others who had hurt him. As Robert forgave each person, he became less angry and better able to deal with his anger when it arose. Robert discovered that there is no closure to the hurts of the past without forgiveness.

Renae saw the change in Robert. He wasn't projecting the blame on her all the time and was taking more responsibility for his actions. His attitude was much more loving, positive and accepting. This encouraged Renae to hang in there and work on her own emotions. She was able to forgive Robert for his past angry behavior and the ways in which he had hurt her. She also worked through her fear regarding Robert's daughter and the mother of his daughter. She began to appropriate God's power, love and stability in her life. She acknowledged how her fear had dominated and negatively affected her relationship with Robert.

Their relationship is working now because they learned how to put God's truth into action—something they took with them into their marriage! Renae and Robert not only learned how to forgive and to receive God's grace for the past, but they also learned how to *communicate with grace*. In chapter 6, we will talk more about how you too can incorporate healing grace into your communication with your spouse and others to bring about lasting change in those relationships.

Refusing Apathy and Choosing Maturity

If you are walking with Jesus hand in hand, do you actually think there would be any needs in your life that would go unmet?

Absolutely not, for God will supply all your needs according to His riches in glory in Christ Jesus (see Phil. 4:19, *KJV*).

One obstacle to letting Jesus have total control is that you may be in such an emotional state that you don't "feel" like doing anything. You may make a quick, emotional decision in hopes of trying anything that might work for you, but the result is usually less than an honest decision and rarely brings about true change. Remember, "As a man thinks in his heart so he is" (Prov. 23:7, *KJV*).

Too many times we rely on old patterns and abilities to deal with problems and relationships. When fear or worry or guilt enters our mind, instead of processing it through the truth of God's Word, we focus on the emotion, which only increases its strength. Instead of seeing the presence of God in a situation, and a solution developing, the problem itself enlarges.

The persistence of negative emotions can lead to hostility and frustration in relationships. Long-term emotions of depression and anxiety can and will result as the body tries to cope through obsessive thoughts, paranoia and fantasy.

But if we focus on Christ and His Word, our mind, will and emotions are healed and strengthened by His power. We will still deal with problems in life, but we can now process them through a heart of grace that has been transformed by truth. Having the mind of Christ is foundational for a new life. Philippians 4:13 states that we can do all things through Christ. This is, of course, the ideal. It is not arrived at immediately. It is not a pill you can take and forever afterward experience the victorious Christian life. It is a day-by-day process of surrender, trust, obedience and growth.

Jane's Story

A young lady in her 20s, Jane was having a rough time in her life. She was depressed and she suffered many physical ailments. Though she came from a Christian family and had accepted Jesus into her life at an early age, she had fallen into the trap of doing life her way.

She married at age 20 against her parents' advice, but she was determined to make it work. She had tried to "save" her husband, but it was obvious that he wanted to be in control. When she rebelled against his controlling ways, he abused her mentally, verbally, emotionally and physically. Though she tried to adjust, sought counseling to work it out and took anti-depressant medication, her marriage ended in divorce. Even after the divorce, she tried to reconcile with her ex-husband, but it still didn't work out. She felt like a failure, and that lowered her self-esteem even more.

Jane was energetic and somewhat optimistic, but self was in control. She went through two more intense romantic relationships. One was a whirlwind courtship, which she thought would result in marriage, but didn't. She gave her all, but it didn't work out. He wanted more of a live-in relationship of intimacy than a commitment to marriage. She took this as more rejection and failure.

Because Jane was an attractive woman, she had no trouble getting attention from men. In another intimate relationship, with a Christian man, which she thought would result in a proposal for marriage, she was once again devastated. This man was too bent on making it big in business. He was striving to become a millionaire and to have it all. Jane went into a deep depression and increased her antidepressant medication.

Many women have a difficult time handling their emotions when they've been hurt. When the men in their life tell them they're worthless and incompetent, many women begin to believe this and it greatly affects their self-esteem. They have a tendency to develop a type of co-dependency, which causes them to continue to hang in there and suffer more abuse. In most cases, it doesn't get better for the woman until, with the help of Christ and a Christian counselor, she finally leaves this kind of relationship for good. And it's when she submits her emotions to the Holy Spirit that she can truly have the grace to control them.

Jane didn't like being so dependent on medication, so she looked for ways to reduce it. She tried natural anti-depressant substitutes with little success. She tried counseling. What worked more than anything else was the presence of Jesus in her life. Once again she sought to grow in her faith. She attended church, read the Bible, read Christian devotionals and spent more time in prayer. She began to ask God to send her a man who would love her as Christ loved the Church and gave Himself for it. She wanted to please God and to trust Him more. She sought to make Jesus her first love. She believed strongly in the return of Jesus and she wanted Him to find her faithful. She wanted to hear Jesus say when He returns, "My grace has saved you and My grace has sustained you."

But she was also hearing Jesus say, "Have you given My grace to those men who have hurt you?" That came as a shock. Jane did some serious soul searching and discovered that she had not fully forgiven all the men who had hurt and disappointed her. She determined that with God's help she would complete what she had started but not finished. With Jesus once again at the center of her life, she was able to complete the healing grace process. She was able to forgive each man in her life so that she could finally have closure.

As Jane forgave each man, she was able to look ahead to her future. She had more joy and peace and felt more of an intimate closeness with Jesus. She began to see how God's grace is truly sufficient. Her self-esteem was renewed and her emotions at peace as she became stronger in the Lord and more hopeful for the future.

It's true. God's grace *is* sufficient, and He wants us to live in grace. His grace is not only sufficient to save us from our sin, but it will also strengthen us in every encounter of our life—in the good times and the bad. He wants us to discover that He loves us so much that He wants not only to be our Savior but also to be the Lord of every aspect of our life.

The Bible has a lot to say about growth, change and maturation. While God loves us just the way we are, He loves us too much to leave us that way. Because He loves us, He wants to see us "become conformed to the image of His son" (Rom. 8:29, *NKJV*). Because He loves us, He wants to help us "grow up in all aspects of Him, who is the head, even Christ" (Eph. 4:15, *NASB*). Because He loves us, He's committed to helping us change.

In 1 Corinthians 3:1, Paul expressed concern over the Corinthian Christians because they hadn't grown. He wrote, "And I, brethren, could not speak to you as to spiritual men, but as to men of flesh, as to babes in Christ" (*NASB*). The writer of Hebrews expressed concern that the readers hadn't changed, they hadn't deepened or matured (see Heb. 5:11-14). He begins chapter 6 by exhorting them to "press on to maturity" (v. 1). What he was really saying was, "Hey, folks, it's time for you to make some changes. It's time for you to grow up."

Our willingness to change, to learn, to grow is God's love language. It tells Him that we believe in Him, we trust Him, we want to be who He wants us to be. Openness to change is our way of taking His hand and following Him. He will never give us more than we can handle (see 1 Cor. 10:13); He can cause all things to work together for good (see Rom. 8:28); and He will supply all of our needs according to His riches in glory (see Phil. 4:19). Therefore, we can let go of fear.

How do we grow up? How do we mature? How do we become who God wants us to be? How do we learn to honor one another, to serve one another, to prefer one another as more important than ourselves?

In 1 Peter 1:7, Peter uses a powerful word picture to describe this process. He compares our lives to gold that is purified by fire. The refining process involves several different "firings" to bring the alloys and impurities to the surface so that the goldsmith can remove them. The refining process takes time, hard work and at times can be painful, but the product is worth it. The end result is pure gold.

Warren Wiersbe said, "We can benefit from change. Anyone who has ever really lived knows that there is no life without growth. When we stop growing, we stop living and start existing. But there is no growth without change, there is no challenge without change. Life is a series of changes that create challenges, and if we are going to make it, we have to grow."[1]

Risking Change

Choosing to change is risky. The word "change" means to make different, to give a different course or direction, to replace one thing with another, to make a shift from one to another, to undergo transformation, transition or substitution. To many people, however, change is negative, something that implies inferiority, inadequacy and failure. To them the prospect of change might feel scary. No wonder so many people resist the idea of change. Who wants to feel inferior and inadequate?

Change is uncomfortable. We resist it even if it's for the better. It involves risk. It's risky to be a risk-taker. I (Norm) know. I've taken a few risks. It's unsettling. It's unnerving. It produces some anxiety because we want to know the outcome of our choices in advance. There is a risk in seeking a new job. What if you're rejected, not just by one potential employer but by several? There is a risk in asking someone out on a date or asking someone to marry you. What if the person says no? That would hurt. But think of the blessing you could miss by not trying, by not asking, by not taking the risk.

I remember the risk of climbing out on a four-inch ledge to creep around a cliff jutting out over the icy water of a high-altitude lake. To add to the difficulty, I had to let go of one handhold to continue creeping along the ledge to reach the next handhold eight feet away. What if my foot slipped and I plunged 20 feet to the frigid water below? It was a risk. But I chose to take that risk to get to the inlet of the lake. It was worth it. Had I given up out of fear, I would have missed out on the joy of catching many brilliant golden trout.

I remember the risk of walking into a bank and asking for a loan of $2,000. It doesn't sound like much, but 34 years ago, when I was earning only $7,000 a year, $2,000 was a very large amount to me. And I was taking a risk. I intended to use the money to publish my own curriculum on marriage. I felt very strongly that this curriculum was needed so that others could teach marriage-enrichment classes in their churches. I felt God's leading coupled with my own convictions. But it still wasn't easy to take out that loan. Where was the assurance that others would buy these books? What if they didn't sell or other people didn't see the same benefit in them that I did?

But I took the risk. The plan was approved. The manuals were printed. They sold, and the monies funded the start-up of a nationwide ministry of training and producing curriculum for churches. The risk was scary, but the blessings enjoyed by thousands of couples over the years have been well worth it.

You say you're not a risk-taker? Everyone is to one degree or other. Perhaps you've just never identified all the risks you've taken in your lifetime. Take a sheet of paper and list several things you once could not do but now are able to do. Begin with very simple items like driving a car. Keep adding to your list for a week. You will be amazed at what you discover. You have grown. You have accomplished much in your life. God has been at work in your life. And everything you learned to do involved a risk. Use this list as a reminder that you are indeed a risk-taker. As you continue to take risks for change and growth, you will discover that you are a blessed person!

When you take a risk, you have to open your hand and loosen your hold on what is certain. You have to reach out for something that is a bit uncertain, but it's usually better than what you have at the present time.

Jesus: Your Answer for Change

Are you ready for change? If the answer to this question is yes, then Jesus says, *Come to Me, take My yoke, learn from Me, find rest for your soul,* for His yoke is easy and His burden is light. Perhaps you're asking the question "What is a yoke?" A yoke is a device used by farmers to keep their pair of oxen from seeking their own way while plowing in a field. Instead of two oxen working against each other and making a mess of the job, they're connected to one another and work together to accomplish the job. They are bound to one another. The younger ox learns from the older one. When we are yoked to Jesus, we learn, grow and change through Him.

Jesus wants you. He has all the grace, gentleness, kindness, wisdom and understanding that you need for change. He has all of these things to give to you and me. He wants you to take up His yoke and learn from Him. Why? Because He cares for us, and He is gentle and humble in heart, and He wants us to find rest for our souls (see Matt. 11:29). He does not want you to lose your way or work against Him. He wants to teach you, help you and train you up in the way you should go. For Jesus says, "I am the way, the truth and the life. No one comes to the Father except through Me" (John 14:6). When you come to Jesus ready for change, you will never be the same.

While in the field of life, being yoked to Jesus will allow you to receive the grace you need for any situation (see 2 Cor. 12:9).

Because He will be tied to you, you will not have to search high and low for Him. You will just have to turn your head and ask Him where you will be going next: "How should I handle this problem, Jesus?"

He wants to be that close to you! This is grace that brings real healing and true transformation! He wants it for you more than you do: He says, "I, even I, am the one who wipes out your transgressions for My own sake; and I will not remember your sins" (Isa. 43:25).

Amazing! God wipes out all of your sins, shortcomings, faults, weaknesses, past hurts and every evil thing that led you to where you are today. Many of those things were not even your own fault. You were the victim of the evil committed by someone else. But your anger, bitterness and resentment have caused you great internal suffering. God can wash all that away. Why? Because He cannot have a relationship with us unless we have received the grace of forgiveness from Jesus so that we can be made more like Him. We also learn, through Jesus, to give others who have hurt us the same grace that God has given freely to us.

Coming to Jesus is not difficult. All you need to do is to answer this question: Are you ready for change?

If the answer is yes, then just ask Jesus, the Change Master, to come into your life and begin to work that work of change through Christ in you. Just like Sarah, who became ready to change, you too can start the journey that will lead you to change.

It took Sarah quite a while to be able to answer the change question in the affirmative. It may take you some time as well. That is okay. Just remember that Jesus is knocking at the door. He never forces change on anyone. Like most of us, you have to be in a position where you recognize that change is required in order for your life to achieve the balance you desire. Then you begin to find true meaning, purpose and fulfillment in life.

If your answer to the question about change is no, then you have other questions to answer: Is your life all that you want it to be? Are you perfectly satisfied with who you are, what you are and with the influence you want to have on your world? Are there nagging weaknesses that you have long desired to be rid of? Are all of your relationships working?

If you are honest with yourself, there are going to be some "no" responses to those questions. In fact, the answer to all of these questions is probably going to be no, or at least a qualified no—that there is room for improvement. In Alcoholics Anonymous and Narcotics Anonymous meetings, step one involves realizing there is a problem and that there is a higher power available for assistance. This higher power is Jesus, and He is still the key to becoming a happy, joyful and free person who is full of peace.

Jesus read the following words from the prophet Isaiah: "'The Spirit of the Lord is on me, because He has anointed me to preach good news to the poor. He has sent me to proclaim freedom for the prisoners and recovery of sight for the blind, to release the oppressed, to proclaim the year of the Lord's favor.' Then he rolled up the scroll, gave it back to the attendant and sat down. The eyes of everyone in the synagogue were fastened on him, and he began by saying to them, 'Today this scripture is fulfilled in your hearing'" (Luke 4:18-21).

With these words, Jesus began His public ministry. Note what Jesus said and what He did not say. He was quoting from

Isaiah 61, but He did not quote it exactly. What He left out is probably as important as what He said. He left out the last part of verse 2, which says, "and the day of vengeance of our God." It's an interesting oversight, or perhaps there was a purpose behind this. Remember that Jesus said, "For God did not send the Son into the world to judge the world; but that the world should be saved through Him" (John 3:17).

Jesus came to do a new thing. He came with grace, mercy and peace. He came to give us life and life more abundant. He came not with a sword but with a word—a word of encouragement, not judgment. This word is the word of life that He wishes for all of us to receive. And this is the foundation for bringing about real change.

Bill's Story

Bill was a tall Texas cowboy in his 40s who was born and raised in the heartland of West Texas. He was a strapping man made in the image of the stereotypical Westerner.

Like many men, Bill had a problem with anger. In fact, his anger was so pronounced that it manifested itself in outbursts of rage, depression and suicidal thoughts. The use of anti-depressants had no apparent positive effect on his anger. After one episode of explosive irritation directed toward his wife, she was so hurt that she confronted him and insisted he go for counseling.

As a young man, Bill suppressed his anger. He became a cowboy and distanced himself from relationships that required intimacy. He partied, sought the company of women and eventually got a woman pregnant. He married her but still kept his distance.

Bill had been born again; however, Jesus was just sitting in the background on the fence, watching him destroy his life because of his unwillingness to surrender to Jesus the things that had led him to such anger and bitterness. Anger was not just the result of repressing feelings of rejection and inferiority. His immoral lifestyle and rebellion were really signs of a man who was unable to face his past hurts.

Bill got to a point where he was so upset with himself that he was suicidal; on top of that he was at great risk of losing the woman he loved—the mother of his children.

Maybe you're like Bill and have come to the point in your life where you are able to say as he did, "It's time. I'm ready for change."

José's Story

José was an 18-year-old Hispanic man who had a problem. Like Bill, this problem was so severe that it threatened the loss of the only thing that mattered to him, his girlfriend. She was a beautiful girl still attending the Christian high school where they met. He knew Jesus as his Savior, yet like many men he relied heavily on himself to meet his needs, take care of problems and be the "man." He thought he was in control of his own life. This senseless pride leads to a separation from Christ. If Christ is no longer in the center of your life, then you are subject to many mistakes that "self" will make along the way.

During an angry outburst, he nearly assaulted the woman he loved. Perhaps his pride was challenged, his manhood questioned, his authority usurped. It doesn't matter what caused the outburst. What did matter was that he took out his anger against her in a verbal rage. This led to a separation and her not wanting to see him again. Although her parents liked José, they said that before he could date her again he had to get professional help.

Have you ever been in a situation where the person (or goal or object) that you valued above all else was about to be removed from your life, not because of some external force or circumstance, but because of your own bitterness, anger and resentment directed toward that person?

Ask yourself, *Where did that anger come from? How am I capable of losing it like that? Why would I risk everything for which I have worked so hard over an outburst of anger? Doesn't pride go before the fall?*

In chapter 5, we'll explore anger and how it leads to problems in relationships. We'll discuss the source of anger and, most important, how to overcome this beast, even as José did.

Okay, I'm ready for change.

Oh, Lord . . . how ready I am for change!

How God's Word Changes Your Thoughts

I *should never have come this morning. I just know that Jack is upset* *with me again. Nothing, absolutely nothing, has gone right lately.* *I wish this depression would go away. I just know something is* *wrong by the way Jack's been acting. I wonder if other people can tell* *how I feel. Why did the pastor choose today to preach on that subject?* *Doesn't he know what that does to me?* The woman's thoughts continue in that vein for the remainder of the service. As she walks out, once again she gives the appearance of being a satisfied, happy person. But we know differently, don't we?

A high school boy sits in the front row, looking very intently at the pastor throughout the service. He must be agreeing with most of what he hears during the hour because he nods in a positive way from time to time. He's smartly dressed and seems to be popular with his peers. He's sought after by several colleges for both his academic and athletic abilities. He seems to have his life together and there is a bright future ahead of him.

Let's tap into his thought life during the church service: *I really feel numb . . . I wonder what the church people will say about me . . . I guess I don't really care. I don't care about anything. I don't know why I'm this way . . . I wonder what the pastor said this morning. I haven't heard a word so far. This is the only way to go . . . I'm never going to be different. I know that others suspect me. They must be talking about me. Well . . . hmm—this will give them something to talk about. Two hours to go . . . two hours to live.*

Self-Talk: The Power of Your Unspoken Words

You would never know the inner thoughts, the inner feelings or the inner turmoil of either of these two people from an outward glance at them. Only God knows the inward feelings and thoughts of the mind. Yet our thought life causes us the most problems.

We all carry on conversations with ourselves daily. We call it self-talk. But are you aware of the importance and impact of this? Self-talk *initiates* and *intensifies* our *emotions*. Self-talk directs the way in which we *behave* toward others. Self-talk determines what we say to others. Self-talk can keep us stuck in our past and sabotage our future.

One major event predisposed us all toward the difficulty we have in life today. The event was what is called the Fall. Adam and Eve listened to Satan and rebelled against God and His way. And because of the Fall, sin entered Adam's and Eve's relationship with God, and imperfection came into our world and exists in many areas of life today.

At the Fall, we lost natural ecological perfection. The natural world is out of balance, manifesting earthquakes, storms, floods, tornadoes, volcanic eruptions, and more.

We lost physical perfection. We are all victims of a gene pool, which becomes increasingly imperfect as deficits are passed from one generation to another.

We lost mental perfection, and in its place we have a bent toward negative or destructive thinking.

We lost emotional perfection. We're out of balance emotionally.

We lost relational perfection. The openness and transparency Adam and Eve enjoyed before the Fall is gone.

We lost spiritual perfection. What was once God-centeredness was replaced by self-centeredness.[1]

So the Fall affects every aspect of our conversation. You and I carry on conversations with ourselves each day. This doesn't mean that we're odd or on the verge of spacing out. It's normal to talk to one's self. After you read this chapter, however, I hope you'll be much more conscious of your self-talk. You'll probably be shocked by the amount of time you spend on inner conversations and how those conversations affect your relationships. Think about this:

What you say to others and how you say it is a direct expression of your self-talk.

What's on the outside reflects what's on the inside.

Self-talk is the message you tell yourself about yourself, others, your experiences, the past, the future, or God. It is a set of evaluating thoughts about facts and events that happen to you. As events are repeated, many of your thoughts, and thus your emotional responses, become almost automatic. Sometimes the words you tell yourself are never put together in clear statements. They may be more like impressions. But they become believable. These silent statements cut a groove in your brain where they are heard most loudly and most often.[2]

Steve's Story

Steve had developed a well-worn groove in his mind and it certainly came out loudly. In counseling he became more aware of his anger and all the hurt, disappointment and rejection he had suffered from his deceased parents. Steve was a Christian and very active in his church, but he had never really dealt with his parent-directed anger. He then started to discover how his anger had hurt not his parents, but his wife and children. The

rejection he felt from his parents had shut him down emotionally, so he was more distant with his family. And since he had a
tendency not to be very involved with them, the pattern of
rejection carried on with them.

His response (self-talk) to this was, "Well, how could I really
give love and acceptance to my wife and children when I never
received it from my family?" This was Steve's reasoning and this
was what Steve had been saying to himself again and again.
It's so easy to become trapped by our words (see Prov. 6:2).
Neurosurgeons have discovered that the speech center in our
brain controls all the nerves in our body—all the more proof
that what we speak is what we get.

Steve is expressing what many men and women have experienced. How can you give something you haven't received?
True, it is difficult to give love and acceptance and to really invest
yourself emotionally in others, especially your spouse and children, if you haven't learned it as a child growing up.

But Steve wanted to be loved and accepted more than anything else by his wife and children, so he was open to dealing
with his past so that he could be healed of the hurts. Though
he had received God's grace through Jesus Christ, he'd never
thought of giving this grace to his parents, as well as his sister,
who was his parent's favorite. His self-talk up to this time had
been, "They don't deserve my forgiveness. Look at what they did
to me. How unfair!" He was a strong, controlling person who also
felt that he had to be in control to keep from being hurt again.

But Steve was determined to give his family this gift of
grace as God had given it to him. It was a moment of truth
when he recognized that his prior forgiveness of them had

been nothing more than a pseudo-forgiveness, a formality that he'd done in his mind but hadn't actualized in his heart. Steve prayed about this and discovered that through Jesus he was able to truly forgive his parents. He said, "It was like Mt. Everest had been lifted off my shoulders."

Steve's self-talk became more positive and gracious. Steve got freed up emotionally to love and accept his wife and children. At first others held back, not knowing when Steve's anger might explode, but within a few months, first his wife and then his three children began to respond to him with love and acceptance in return.

Steve's oldest daughter, Sherry, who lived in another country, heard of the change in her father from her mother and siblings, so she decided to come home and see for herself. Sherry's self-talk was, "Dad will never change. I'll just keep my distance and not be hurt anymore." After hearing from her mom and siblings, her self-talk changed to, "Maybe Dad has changed. I would really like to have a relationship with him."

It was moving to see Steve and his daughter begin to relate to each other in a loving way for perhaps the first time. Sherry opened up to giving grace to her father, having herself developed a relationship with Jesus. In one counseling session, Sherry came and sat on her father's lap, something she had missed while growing up. They cried and hugged each other. Sherry said how this fulfilled her hope and dream that one day she and her father would be able to reconcile and love each other.

Steve and Sherry rejoiced in having their newfound relationship. Their self-talk was now about thanking God.

Based on Your Beliefs

Self-talk (your inner conversation) usually is not an emotion or feeling. Self-talk can be equated with your evaluating thoughts. Your expression of anger, your ways of showing love, and how you handle conflict are all driven by self-talk. You might be aware of it, and then again you might not. Your self-talk may be based upon some of your attitudes. A positive attitude toward life tends to generate positive self-talk, while a negative attitude generates negative self-talk. Self-talk is *based* on your beliefs. And what you truly believe is manifested both in your inner and oral conversations.

Most of the people we have talked with believe that outside events, other people and circumstances determine their emotions, behaviors and verbal responses. Those things certainly influence us, but it's our thoughts that are usually the source of how we feel and behave and speak. Even if our thoughts are irrational, we tend to believe them. What we think about these things and about people will determine the emotions we feel and the behaviors and verbal responses we express. We prefer to think others are the problem, because it's easier to blame than to say, "It's me." Instead we say, "I'm right and you're wrong. I'm not the one who needs to change."

As an example of how your beliefs affect your self-talk, consider these typical beliefs about marriage:

1. My spouse should make me happy.
2. My spouse should meet all my needs.
3. My spouse should know what my needs are without my having to tell him/her.

4. My spouse should be willing to do things according to my way of doing them.

5. My spouse should not respond in an irritable or angry way to me.

Do these statements reflect self or grace?

If you have any of these beliefs, each will lead to one thought after another, each one more intense, more inflammatory and more stress producing than the one before. In fact, many people carry on imaginary conversations between themselves and the other person to the extent they may believe the conversation actually took place! Sound familiar?

Here are some typical thoughts that will probably enter your mind at one time or another:

"My spouse will never change. He/she will always be that kind of person."

"I can never meet my spouse's needs."

"If I bring up that subject, my spouse will just get mad again."

"If I share what really happened, I'll never be trusted again."

"Why bother asking him/her to share his/her feeling? He/she will only clam up again."

"He hates me."

"I just know there's an affair going on."

"He's so inconsiderate! Why doesn't he grow up?"

"I must have everything perfect in my house."

These are thoughts I've heard from many people. What do you think each statement would do to your emotional state? To your relationship with the other person?

Self-talk generates and creates mental pictures in our mind. As mental pictures begin to emerge, our imagination is called into action. As we run mental pictures through the panoramic screen of our mind, our self-talk is expanded and reinforced.

How Do You Think?

Do you sit around thinking about what you are going to think next? Of course not! Thoughts slide into our consciousness so smoothly that we don't even sense their entrance. Many thoughts are stimulated by past experience, attitudes and beliefs. We build storehouses of memories and experience, retaining and remembering those things on which we concentrate the most.

Whether they're automatic or consciously thought out, what are your thoughts? Are they negative or positive? Most people who worry or are depressed, irritable or critical toward others have thoughts that are automatically negative.

A characteristic of negative thoughts is that they're generally wrong. They don't reflect reality, but they do reflect our insecurity, our feelings of inadequacy and our fears. These alien invaders shouldn't be welcome guests in our mind. They're generally exaggerated negative conclusions about our future, our spouse, our marriage, our life, ourselves. These kinds of thoughts cripple us. Look at the following list and see if any describe your thinking process.

1. *All-or-nothing thinking.* A person who thinks this way sees everything in black-or-white terms. No shades of gray are even possible. Perfectionists see their

work as either perfect or worthless. But a balanced person sees variations and exceptions in nearly every area of life.

2. *Over-generalization.* This is a tendency to draw sweeping conclusions from very little evidence. A healthy thinker draws conclusions only after taking in a great deal of evidence.

3. *Negative mental filter.* Filtering out information that is positive or good, this person tends not to hear compliments or words of affirmation or praise. Instead, he or she hears only criticism. A healthy person hears both good and bad. Included in this would be disqualifying the positive; in other words, hearing the compliment but discounting it. This person explains away any words of affirmation or praise.

4. *Jumping to conclusions.* This is a common problem. It's when we believe we know what other people are thinking about us. We think we're mind readers. Assuming that we know the thoughts of others is the cause of many sad misunderstandings.

5. *Magnification/minimization.* This is when someone exaggerates the importance of isolated events or encounters. You might magnify your own emotions, mistakes or imperfections and minimize any success you might have.

6. *Emotional reasoning.* This is when you see an outcome as directly coming from your emotions. For example, you may feel hopeless about passing an exam, so you don't show up to take it.

7. *"Should" statements.* This is another common mind disease in which one has a rigid set of internal rules about what should, must, ought, can't and has to be done.

8. *Labeling.* This is when we tend to give ourselves or others negative labels such as "stupid," "imbecile" or "loser."

9. *Personalization.* Personalization is marked by an inclination to blame yourself for events over which you have no control or less control than you assume.[3]

Do you identify with any of these? Let's look a little further into our thought life. If you look up the word "slander" in the dictionary, you'll find that it's the utterance of a false statement, or statements, that are damaging to a third person's character or reputation.[4] Many of our thoughts about one another fall into this category.

Many spouses slander each other in their minds. Many parents as well as children do the same. I have heard many such comments in my counseling office. And this character-assassination style of thinking generates both conflict and distance in marriage, family and other relationships. When we think slanderously, we're not responding out of grace, nor are we offering grace.

Have you ever met an assassin? Probably not. An assassin has one job and one goal in mind—to kill. While very few spouses ever physically assassinate their mates, many assassinate them in their minds. As a result, the spouse's character is torn down. Character assassination is a root cause of many marital difficulties. On the other hand, if you respond in a positive way in your mind, the way you act and speak will be different.[5]

All too often, the problem with what you say to one another (and usually regret later) is a result of minutes or even hours of talking to yourself about your spouse or the situation. Often these thoughts hop in automatically and camouflage themselves amidst other thoughts. The authors of *We Can Work It Out* call these "hot thoughts" and best describe the thoughts this way:

> Hot thoughts lead to feelings of hopelessness ("He's never going to change"), anger and resentment ("I don't deserve to be treated like this"), and even depression ("All I want to do is stay in bed, watch TV and eat"). Hot thoughts also lead directly to destructive patterns of relationship talk. If you feel angry and hopeless, you will say things that communicate these feelings. You are likely to criticize your partner, offer negative problem solutions, mind-read your partner's thoughts and feelings, and fail to utilize listening talk. Because these behaviors tend to elicit replies in kind from your partner, you find yourself in the middle of an argument that confirms your worst thoughts. But it's a vicious cycle. Your thoughts lead to actions that increase the chance

of conflict, and the inevitable conflicts provide energy for more hot thoughts. You will rapidly find yourself trapped in one or more of the now-familiar patterns of escalation and pursuit—withdrawal.[6]

Do you see how hurtful hot thoughts are and why they should be avoided? In order to avoid these thoughts, strive to adore your partner's character rather than assassinate it. Adoring your spouse in your mind will build a positive and healthy thought life, which in turn will produce a growing, fulfilling marriage relationship.

Let's put it this way: Whatever happens within a marriage relationship reflects the inner workings of each person's mind and heart, whether positive or negative. Do your thoughts fall more in the "self" category or the "grace" category? Positive or negative relationships (be they with your spouse, parent, child, friend, co-worker, and so forth) become a choice—your choice.

Max Lucado shared the story of the world's most unwanted ship, the *Pelicano*. No country in the world wanted her. No country allowed her to land. She was a seaworthy ship and had reputable owners.

The problem was that she was filled with 15,000 tons of trash. It ranged from orange peelings to beer bottles to newspaper and dozens of other items. She was filled with the 1986 summer trash from Philadelphia. That's when the municipal workers went on strike and the trash piled higher and higher. No one wanted it. The owners of the *Pelicano* thought they could make money by transporting it elsewhere. But no one wanted it. It was too much and then too old and now possibly toxic.

No one wants a trash-filled ship. Very few want those in their life whose mind and heart are filled with trash.[7] Trash contaminates our relationships. Think of it this way:

Today's thoughts are tomorrow's acts.
Today's bigotry is tomorrow's hate crime.
Today's anger is tomorrow's abuse.
Today's lust is tomorrow's adultery.
Today's greed is tomorrow's embezzlement.
Today's fear is tomorrow's reality.

Some folks don't know we have an option. Listening to our vocabulary, you'd think we are the victims of our own thoughts.[8]

Do you think we have a choice of what thoughts we entertain or invite in? Paul says we do: "We capture every thought and make it give up and obey Christ" (2 Cor. 10:5, NCV). Our task is to face every thought and say, "Hold it right there. You are not allowed into *my* mind!"

Max Lucado went on to say, "What if you did that? What if you took every thought captive? What if you refused to let any trash enter your mind? What if you took the counsel of Solomon, 'Be careful what you think because your thoughts run your life' (Prov. 4:23, NCV)?"[9]

You are not a victim of your thoughts. You have a vote; you have a voice. You can exercise thought prevention. You can also exercise thought permission.[10] Remember, your thoughts turn into your actions.

Mind Makeover

What about God's Word? What does He say about our thoughts? Scriptures have much to say about thinking and the thought life. The words "think," "thought" and "mind" are used more than 300 times in the Bible. The book of Proverbs says, "As he thinks within himself, so he is" (Prov. 23:7, *NASB*).

What does Scripture say about our inner conversations or self-talk?

Scripture indicates that our mind is often the basis for the difficulties and problems that we experience. Romans 8:6-7 states, "Now the mind of the flesh [which is sense and reason without the Holy Spirit] is death—death that comprises all the miseries arising from sin, both here and hereafter. But the mind of the (Holy) Spirit is life and soul-peace . . . [That is] because the mind of the flesh—with its carnal thoughts and purposes— is hostile to God" (*AMP*).

God knows the content of our thoughts: "All the ways of a man are pure in his own eyes, but the Lord weighs the spirit— the thoughts and intents of the heart" (Prov. 16:2, *AMP*). Also, "The Word of God is full of living power. It is sharper than the sharpest knife, cutting deep into our innermost thoughts and desires. It exposes us for what we really are" (Heb. 4:12, *NLT*).

A Christian does not have to be dominated by the thinking of the old mind, the old pattern. We have been set free! God has not given us the spirit of fear, but of power, and of love, and of a sound mind (see 2 Tim. 1:7). Soundness means that the new mind can think rightly, in a way that honors God, ourselves and others.

Are you aware that all of us need an "extreme makeover" when it comes to our thought life? It's true. It's interesting that our culture is makeover crazy when it comes to physical appearance, and it's amazing the number of people who are willing to put themselves under the knife for a nip and tuck.

A friend describes what God wants for us:

Did you know that God has chosen you for an "extreme makeover"? Most of us come to the Word of God looking for advice to help us fix ourselves up a little, only to discover that God wants to do something far more dramatic and intense. He wants to penetrate the dark corners of our inner lives and deal with the thoughts and attitudes of our hearts and transform us into a people who radiate his beauty and grace. This makeover is a painful, lifelong process, and the tool God often uses is his Word, which cuts deeply and lays bare the ugliness we might wish to keep hidden. Then he begins his work of cutting away what is keeping us from displaying the beauty of his presence in our lives. And the cutting away is painful.[11]

What can you do to make over your mind? Let your mind be filled with the *mind of Christ*. Scripture encourages us that we can do this! In Philippians 2:5, Paul commands, "Let this mind be in you, which was also in Christ Jesus" (*KJV*). This could be translated, "Be constantly thinking this in yourselves, or reflect in your own minds *the mind of Christ Jesus*." The meaning here for the words "this mind be" is "to have understanding, to be wise, to direct one's mind to a thing, to seek or strive for."

Understand that, in God's eyes, what's going on in our minds carries the same weight as how we behave. At times Scripture uses the word "heart" where we would use the word "mind," as in "apply your heart to discipline" (Prov. 23:12, *NASB*). In the New Testament, Jesus used the word "heart" in the same sense: "And Jesus knowing their thoughts said, 'Why are you thinking evil in your *hearts?*'" (Matt. 9:4, *NASB*).

God is looking at our mind, into our heart. We're to have the mind of Christ. We are called to become more and more like God: "Put on the new self, created to be like God in true righteousness and holiness" (Eph. 4:24). The purpose of the new self is Godlikeness. Paul said to the Colossians, "You have to put on the new self, which is being renewed in knowledge in the image of its Creator" (Col. 3:10). How can you do this? You can't. You can't do it on your own, that is. But by the power of the Holy Spirit and the washing of our minds with the Word, we can conform to Christ's image.

Consider the following verses:

"For the mind set on the flesh is death, but the mind set on the Spirit is *life* and peace" (Rom. 8:6, emphasis added). God wants our mind to be alive. A mind that's alive chooses the Scriptures as its standard and receives direction from God. We make choices with our mind that cause us to grow and to reflect God's grace in our response to others.

To what extent is your mind alive in this way?

He also desires for us to have a mind that is at *peace*: "The mind set on the spirit is life and *peace*" (Rom. 8:6, emphasis added). And God's peace can be there in the midst of chaos and turmoil.

Perhaps you've watched runners or swimmers as they compete. Part of their instruction before hearing the word "go" is the word "set." They assume a certain posture, holding it for all they're worth and with intensity to block out anything else. We're called to keep our minds "set."

To what extent is your mind set in this way?

We're also called to be single-minded rather than distracted. Paul wrote, "But I am afraid, lest as the serpent deceived Eve by his craftiness, your minds should be led astray from the simplicity and purity of devotion to Christ" (2 Cor. 11:3, *NASB*). It's easy to get our minds sidetracked or led astray. What we focus on enlarges. What are you focusing on?

To what extent are you single-minded in this way?

Another godly standard for our mind is found in Philippians 2:3: "Do nothing out of selfish ambition or vain conceit, but in humility consider others better than yourselves." We're called to have a humble mind. We don't build ourselves up, or as some have said, "become legends in our own mind." This humility comes about through submission to the will of God. The mind of Christ knows God and submits to Him.

We are told in 1 Peter 1:13 to gird up our minds. This takes mental effort, a decision to hone in our thoughts on God and put out of our minds anything that would hinder us. Thoughts of worry, fear, lust, hate, jealousy and unwillingness must be brought to the Cross. This includes negative and unrealistic self-talk too. Instead, "whatever is true, whatever is honorable, whatever is right, whatever is pure, whatever is lovely, whatever is of good repute, if there is any excellence and if anything worthy of praise, let your mind dwell on these things" (Phil. 4:8, *NASB*). When we do this, grace will flourish in our lives.

To what extent is your mind humble in this way?

Purity is another one of God's standards for our mind. Titus 1:15 states, "To the pure, all things are pure; but to those who are defiled and unbelieving, nothing is pure, but both their mind and their conscience are defiled" (*NASB*). This verse implies that purity is the redeemed state of the Christian mind. But it's difficult to maintain given the onslaught of opposing input we encounter each day. If you want a pure mind, then you need to know ahead of time what you will do when temptation comes your way. The act of overcoming is a work in progress, not a spur-of-the-moment decision. This is why memorizing Scripture is so helpful.

To what extent is your mind alive in this way? The more alive our mind is in these areas, the more we can respond with grace. The more we sift our thoughts through the Word, the more God's grace can abound in our life.

On the evening of the resurrection, when Jesus appeared to the disciples, the Gospels say that He opened their mind to understand the Scriptures. He opened their minds so that they were *responsive* and *sensitive* to God. We will grow and respond in grace the more the Word of God is active in our life. As we look to it for guidance, for clarification, for decision-making and for guiding our very words, we make our minds alive to it. This requires going through life and asking, "What does God's Word say about this?" and then following it.[12]

As one author summed up this characteristic, "As the Father is to the Son so Christ is to us. He saw the activity of the Father; we pay close attention to the known earthly activity of Jesus. He heard from the Father; we must hear from Him. The Father taught Him; He teaches us. He could do nothing independently of Him. He was very close to the Father; we must remain close to Him; pray that God will make you more sensitive to Him."[13]

To what extent is your mind responsive and sensitive to God?

Paul challenged followers of Christ, "Do not be conformed to this world, but be transformed by the renewing of your mind, that you may prove what is that good and acceptable and perfect will of God" (Rom. 12:2). Part of experiencing a spiritual renewal in your mind is to make a conscious choice that you will change what you put into your mind and, therefore, change your thought patterns.

John Hagee once said, "Watch your thoughts, for they will become your words. Choose your words, for they become actions. Understand your actions, for they become habits. Study your habits, for they will become your character; for it becomes your destiny."[14]

Another way to eliminate automatic negative thoughts is to learn to counter or answer them. Countering means bringing your thoughts to trial and examining the evidence. But you can do this only if you are aware of them. You need to catch the thoughts that come into your mind, and then, when you are aware of them, respond with a conscious positive thought. You don't have to settle for negative thinking. You can choose what you will think about.

One way to determine if your thoughts are helping or hurting is to keep a journal of all the ways in which your thinking may have become distorted or self-sabotaging. Listen to yourself. Every time you hear yourself drawing a conclusion that may reflect any of the nine thinking patterns—write it down.

Then go back through your journal entries and, next to each distorted thought, write a verse or short passage from the Bible that addresses that perception.

Then confess to God that you have allowed yourself to believe those distorted thoughts. Ask Him to set you free from the bondage that these lies have created in you.

Memorize the verses that you have written down in your journal. These are the verses you'll want to meditate on and quote in order to keep this type of thinking from continuing to take root and dig a deeper rut in your mind. Perhaps the following could be yours:

- I can do all things through Christ who strengthens me (Phil. 4:13).

- Thanks be to God who always leads us in triumph in Christ (2 Cor. 2:14).

- My God shall supply all your need according to His riches in glory by Christ Jesus (Phil. 4:19).

- Do not think it strange concerning the fiery trial which is to try you . . . but rejoice to the extent that you partake of Christ's sufferings, that when His glory is revealed, you may also be glad with exceeding joy (1 Pet. 4:12-13).

- Trust in the Lord with all your heart, and lean not on your own understanding; In all your ways acknowledge Him, And He shall direct your paths (Prov. 3:5-6).

- Forgetting those things which are behind and reaching forward to those things which are ahead, I press toward the goal for the prize of the upward call of God in Christ Jesus (Phil. 3:13-14).

- Do not be deceived, God is not mocked; for whatever a man sows, that he will also reap (Gal. 6:7).

- He sent His word and healed them, and delivered them from their destructions (Ps. 107:20).

- Bless the Lord, O my soul, and forget not all His benefits: Who forgives all your iniquities, Who heals all your diseases, Who redeems your life from destruction, Who crowns you with lovingkindness and tender mercies (Ps. 103:2-4).

- Let us not grow weary while doing good, for in due season we shall reap if we do not lose heart (Gal. 6:9).

- My grace is sufficient for you, for my strength is made perfect in your weakness, therefore glory in your weakness that the power of Christ may rest upon you (2 Cor. 12:9).[15]

With practice you can learn to turn your thoughts off and on. To do so you must put things in their proper perspective. The more a person practices control, the greater the possibility of immediate control. We do not have to act in accordance with our self-talk or our feelings.

Is self-control of negative self-talk the answer to changing wrong patterns of thinking? Yes and no. By itself, no. It is a means or a tool. Without assistance, none of us has the capability to extract the negative thoughts and images from our minds. Colossians 3:15 states, "And let the peace of Christ rule in your hearts." The person of Jesus Christ is the answer. Jesus Himself wants us to be open about our thought life and the inner images that are there. All aberrant thoughts should be brought to Christ (see 2 Cor. 10:5). By sharing them with Him and asking Him for strength through the ministry of the Holy Spirit, change will occur.

Prayer

We have available to us unbelievable resources for change and growth and stability. But we need to avail ourselves of these resources by conversing with God and allowing Him to talk to us directly as well as through His Word.

When you pray, how do you do it? Is it a natural experience for you? Do you use your own language and style of talking, or do you feel that you have to talk in a certain manner or phrasing in order to get through?

What we pray about is personal, but I'd like to recommend one specific prayer: Ask God to refashion your thinking. This begins by consecrating your imagination and thought life to God and asking Him to cleanse your thought life of anything that would hinder your growth and progress in life. This suggestion is in keeping with a passage of Scripture found in 1 Peter 1:13: "Gird up . . . mind" (*KJV*). "Gird" means to surround, enclose or hem in. As believers, the Holy Spirit can give us greater awareness of the thoughts that control our lives and greater access to the specific thoughts that need to be changed. With God's assistance, we can develop a much greater sensitivity to our inner dialogue.

As I (Larry) have asked people in counseling to commit their inner dialogues to God each day, I have also asked, "How do you envision God responding to admission of your thoughts and pattern of thinking?" This usually provokes not only an interesting response but an indication of the person's image of God.

Here again our negative inner dialogues have kept us from honest expression—with God. We don't have to fear. He won't be surprised or amazed or shocked by anything we say to Him, since He is already aware of our thoughts anyway: "When far away you know my every thought" (Ps. 119:2, *TLB*).

How do we pray then? First we come to God and admit that our thought lives need renewal and changing. Next, if we lack that desire, we envision Jesus Christ as willing to help us develop the desire to change our thoughts. Often people find it helpful to start the day by asking God to help them identify and dissect their thoughts and then reassemble them. Scripture tells us to "bring every thought into captivity to the obedience of Christ" (2 Cor. 10:5, *NKJV*). This step moves us toward having the mind of Christ.

Pray for the desire to be rid of the old pattern of thinking. Invite Jesus Christ into your thought life and allow the Holy Spirit into the depths of your imagination to bring to light any images or thoughts that are creating a barrier. It is safe to do this in the presence of Jesus Christ and with His strength and comfort. During this prayer time, when a troublesome thought or image comes to mind, see yourself taking it in your hands and giving it to the Lord.

James's life is an example of how you can overcome the old mind and way of thinking and even break the pattern of identification with Mom and Dad and change it to identification with Christ. James was asked to meditate on the following verse day and night: "If any man is in Christ he is a new creation; the old has passed away, behold the new has come" (2 Cor. 5:17, *RSV*). He really took this to heart. He literally memorized the verse, meditated on it and internalized it.

After two weeks he came back to the clinic a changed man. He no longer saw himself only as a son of Mom and Dad, but also as a son of the living God, a joint-heir of Jesus Christ (see Rom. 8:1-18). He was able to see himself as being of immeasurable, magnificent and infinite worth.

James was truly a new person in Christ, the old things (including identification with Mom and Dad) were gone. All things (including a new identification with Jesus Christ) were made new (see 2 Cor. 5:17, *RSV*).

Now through this identification with Christ, James could forgive his mom and dad. God's grace enabled him to love and forgive his parents and to pass that grace on to them. James could let go of the past as he had been healed of his heartache, pain, anger and disappointment. He was able to reach out for the great future God had for him. He could press on toward the mark of the high calling of God in Jesus Christ (see Phil. 3:13-14).

Some people find it helpful as they pray to lift one hand to their head. Imagine placing your destructive thought in that hand, and then reaching forward and placing it in Jesus' outstretched hands. The physical movement, along with the prayer, has a greater sense of reality to it and strengthens motivation. This type of praying takes time and often needs to be repeated for each image or thought that emerges. This is not to say that these thoughts will never return, but now the person will be able to confront them in a new way. As Martin Luther said, we can't stop the birds from flying over our heads, but we can stop them from building a nest in our hair!

This approach, aligned with the reworking of self-talk and the use of prayer, can bring about what Isaiah has assured us: "You will keep in perfect peace him whose mind is steadfast, because he trusts in you" (Isa. 26:3).

Here is a prayer that may assist you:

Lord, I am at the place of asking You to take over my thought life, my inner dialogues, and my imagination and not only clean them up but give me the power to control my thoughts. I am learning which thoughts cause me the most grief and which ones help me. I have to admit to You that I am a creature of habit, and I know I have spent years developing this type of negative thinking. I do want to communicate better with others and with myself and I need Your help. I ask You to cause me to be very aware of what I am thinking and its effect. Please remind me and I will respond to Your prodding. If I revert back to my old way of thinking from time to time, help me not to fall back into being negative about myself because of this lapse. Help me to be patient with myself and with You. Thank You for hearing me and accepting me; and thank You for what You will do for my thought life and inner dialogues in the future.

Try praying this out loud each day for a month and notice the difference. And remember, "God's grace is sufficient for me and His strength is made perfect in my weakness; therefore I will glory in my weakness that the power of Christ may rest upon me" (adapted from 2 Cor. 12:9).

CHAPTER 6

From Anger to Forgiveness—
Grace in Action

Remember Bill? He was the likable cowboy with a pleasant personality who eventually realized that his whole life was a façade. He knew how to play the game to be accepted by others. He had a problem, however, that made him like a walking time bomb. That problem was anger.

He had romanticized the cowboy life in his mind, which allowed him to stay carefree. It gave him a license to drink and carouse. Though he called himself a Christian, he didn't maintain a Christian lifestyle. He didn't spend enough time with God to be changed. Like many men, he tried to do it all through self.

What Is Anger, and What Do You Do with It?

What do you know about anger? It's a controversial, misunderstood word and emotion. It affects all of us, yet continues to baffle us. Even so-called experts disagree. Some say, "Experience it and express it." Others say, "Disown it and repel it." But we all feel anger at times whether we like it or not. God created us with emotions, and one of those is anger.

One dictionary calls anger "a feeling of strong displeasure."[1] How would you describe it? The dictionary definition suggests that anger is manageable, that it is like so many other feelings—neither right nor wrong in itself. The problem lies in its mishandling.

Some people express their anger like a heat-seeking missile. There is no warning. No alarms sound. Everything has been calm, and then the missile explodes. The damage can include wounded feelings and distanced relationships, and the recovery from the onslaught can take a long time.

For other people, anger is a snake gliding silently and unseen through the underbrush. It may raise its head once in a while but then it disappears again, only to strike when someone gets too close for comfort. Or the anger may slink by as a lot of weak excuses that cause costly delays. The bite of this anger is not as blatant or devastating as the latter, but the results can be similar. Is this anyone you know?

Consider some of the destructive results of this emotion: Anger can motivate you to hate, wound, damage, annihilate, despise, scorn, loathe, vilify, curse, ruin and demolish. When you're angry you might ridicule, get even with, laugh at, humiliate, shame, criticize, bawl out, fight, crush, offend or bully another person. You might go to extremes in handling your anger, whether you suppress it or express it. Turn it outward too much and it destroys others; turn it inward too much and it destroys you.

Almost everything in life has a price tag. Go into any store and rarely will you find anything free. Purchasing a new car may give a feeling of elation, comfort and prestige, but you have to pay for those feelings. In the same way, expressing your anger can be a relief—it can influence or even control a situation—but it too has a price tag. These costs might include a strained relationship (resistance or withdrawal of others when you come near them), or even a tension-filled relationship with a spouse who is a combatant rather than a lover.

Anger easily turns from irritation to resentment and bitterness, which can eat away at our body. When we cling to angry memories, we risk detrimental results. Don Colbert, M.D, the author of *Deadly Emotions*, said, "There is very little, if any, love in the person who reflects extreme bitterness, resentment, anger, and hate. Hatred demands more and more emotional space until it crowds out all positive emotions."[2] Even though there are personal physiological costs to anger, the greatest price to be paid is in our interpersonal relationships. Anger never draws a person closer—it always pushes him or her farther away.

Anger has its place because it can sometimes be constructive, but usually it's destructive. Anger, carelessly expressed, will override the love, care and appreciation that create close relationships. The person who has a reputation for anger is given a wide berth. The book of Proverbs recommends, "Make no friendships with a man given to anger, and with a wrathful man do not associate, lest you learn his ways and get yourself into a snare" (22:24-25, *AMP*).

What's Under that Anger?

Is it possible to be angry and yet not sin? Ephesians 4:26-27 indicates that it is: "Be angry and yet do not sin. Do not let the sun go down on your anger, and do not give the devil an opportunity." Notice the second part of the verse. What kind of opportunity is the devil looking for? What interests the devil? John 10:10 says that the thief comes to "steal, kill and destroy." He wants to steal our joy, love, peace and happiness. If we give him an opportunity, he can use anger to destroy relationships between God and man, man and woman, parent and child, siblings, friends, pastors and church members, co-workers and so on.

Lashing out in anger opens the door for our enemy. Reaching out in humility, however, opens the door for Christ and His grace to work in our hearts. Ephesians 4:32 says it so well: "Be ye kind to one another, tenderhearted [not hard-hearted], forgiving one another as God in Christ has forgiven you" (*KJV*). This is what we're called to do.

Angry feelings can clue us in to underlying attitudes. They can tell us that something is wrong. Anger may be the first emotion we are aware of, but it is rarely the first emotion we experience in a particular situation. The emotions that most frequently precede anger are *fear, hurt* or *frustration*. Not only are these feelings painful, but they also drain us of energy and increase our sense of vulnerability.

Remember when Jesus looked at the Pharisees with anger? The passage states that He was "grieved at their hardness of heart" (Mark 3:5, *NASB*). He was *hurt*, which led to anger.

Fear also causes anger. When we are afraid of something, we often don't act afraid but instead become angry. Sometimes anger is a more comfortable emotion than fear. Perhaps it is because we are on the offensive rather than the defensive. We sometimes use anger as a defense to hide behind when we're afraid for others to see what we're really like inside. Unfortunately, that confuses others and they, in turn, may become angry. In most cases, anger begets anger.

Frustration often leads to anger when our expectations are not being fulfilled or when we're not getting our way. When we focus on our frustrations, our thought life or self-talk can feed anger as well.

Now, what can we do to deal with our anger? What choices are available to us?

Anger's Many Faces

There are four basic ways most people deal with anger. The first way is by *repressing* it—never admitting that they are angry, simply ignoring its presence. This repression is often unconscious, but it is *not* healthy. Repressing anger is like placing a wastebasket full of paper in a closet and setting fire to it. The fire will either burn itself out or will set the whole house on fire. The energy produced by anger cannot be destroyed. It must be converted or directed into another channel.

A second way people handle anger is by *suppressing* it—aware of anger, but choosing to hold it in and not let others know about it. In some situations this may be wise, but eventually anger needs to be recognized and drained away in a healthy manner. The person who always stuffs anger away is a sad case. The constant effort of keeping it in is an incredible waste of energy. Though their cheerful, smiling exteriors make it seem otherwise, these "stuffers" are usually very unhappy people. Some stuffers literally stuff themselves by eating enormous amounts of food, partly as a way of punishing themselves for the "sin of anger" (as they sometimes perceive it).

Suppressing anger does have some merit, however, especially if it allows you time to relax, cool down and act in a rational manner. The Word of God has a few things to say about this type of suppression:

- He who is slow to anger has great understanding, but he who is hasty of spirit exposes and exalts his folly (Prov. 4:29, *AMP*). (This person suppresses strife in the beginning so that it doesn't break out.)

- He who is slow to anger is better than the mighty, and he who rules his own spirit than he who takes a city (Prov. 16:32, *AMP*).

- Good sense makes a man restrain his anger, and it is his glory to overlook a transgression or an offense (Prov. 19:11, *AMP*).

- A [self-confident] fool utters all his anger, but a wise man keeps it back and stills it (Prov. 29:11, *AMP*). (This person does not give unbridled license to his anger, but sort of hushes it up, puts it in the background and overcomes it.)

- I [Nehemiah] was very angry when I heard their cry and these words. I thought it over and then rebuked the nobles and officials (Neh. 5:6-7, *AMP*). (Nehemiah took a step back to consider his anger. One version translates this verse as "I consulted with myself.")

Expressing anger is another way to handle it. Some people think you should express exactly how you feel no matter what or who is involved. They feel this is psychologically healthy and necessary in order to live a balanced life. But expressing anger is not getting rid of it. Doing that depends on *how* you express it. Is it with grace and self-control or with spite and a desire to "sock it to" the other person?

There's a fourth way to handle anger, and that is to *turn it down*. If on a scale of 1 to 10 your anger is a 9, turn it down to

1 or 2. You can do this by taking time out and changing your beliefs as well as your self talk. Then you will be able to transform anger into grace and forgiveness.

But how do you accomplish this?

Perhaps José's and Bill's stories will give us some clues.

José's Story Revisited

When José was told that in order to experience peace and move beyond his anger, he would have to release his parents from their offenses against him, thereby forgiving them, he said, "No way!" The anger he had toward them was so strong, he could not forgive them. Ironically, the people who seek to experience peace in their lives, who suffer from this devastating emotion of anger, cannot see that it's their inability to forgive that blocks them from the healing they so desperately need and desire.

Only by the grace of God through Jesus can this be accomplished. Although José had received Jesus as Savior, like many of us he still had not been able to acknowledge Jesus as Lord and give Him full control of his life. When he discovered that Christ, who forgave him of all of his offenses, had empowered him to forgive others, especially his mother and father, José began to achieve victory over anger.

Christ has to be in the center of your existence if you desire to be set free. Self must be put to death to allow the life and grace of God to be expressed through us (see 2 Cor. 12:9). José needed to be able to say, "Dad, I forgive you for being absent in my life, for not being there for me. You lacked the life that I now have. I forgive you." Once he was able to forgive his father, it became easier for him to forgive his mother. When that happened, José felt the weight finally removed from his shoulders.

You too can experience the incredible release from emotional and spiritual bondage that accompanies anger, bitterness and resentment. Jesus came to proclaim freedom to prisoners and liberty to captives. The only thing that can get in the way of freedom is pride and unbelief. Don't let doubt or prideful unwillingness get in the way of forgiving others and acknowledging Jesus' ability to do a miracle in your heart.

For José, forgiving his mother was not enough. He wanted to put that emotion into action, for faith without works is dead (see Gal. 2:20). So he called his mother. She was surprised, maybe a bit embarrassed as well, but she agreed to get together. The grace José had experienced and the love of God allowed him to spend some meaningful moments with her. She saw how God had worked in his life. As a recipient of grace, José was able to see his mother through the eyes of grace, listen to her through the ears of grace, speak to her with a tongue of grace and, finally, to feel for her with a heart of grace.

The transformation process that can occur in us involves learning and spiritual growth, and is the result of learning who God is and spending time in His presence. As His Word takes root in us and the Holy Spirit fills us, we are changed. It is a daily process. As we read in Romans, "we all, with unveiled face beholding as in a mirror the glory of the Lord, are being transformed into the same image from glory to glory, just as from the Lord, the Spirit" (12:2).

Bill's Story Revisited

Bill reluctantly came to the place where he could share about his past hurts. Bill's hurt came from his parents, who made him feel inadequate and worthless. Their words and their actions hurt deeply, and in Bill, that hurt gave birth to anger. He may have been tough as nails on the outside, but on the inside he was a tender person. Tears came to his eyes as he shared that he loved people and loved the Lord, but he did not love his parents or himself.

Church, however, was not the "cowboy" thing to do, so Bill found many excuses to not attend. Every excuse drew him a step farther away from the Lord. He had always been in charge of his own life, but there came a point when he realized he was making a complete mess of it. Jesus needed to be in the saddle. Only by surrendering to Christ could he truly understand and forgive himself and his parents.

Has your heart become hardened to protect yourself from further hurt, just like Bill's and José's?

If so, it's time for you to follow in their footsteps and realize that only Jesus can ease the pain, forgive you and give you the desire and power to forgive those who have hurt you. We'll take a closer look at the process of forgiveness later in this chapter.

The Courage to Believe and Forgive

Remember Sarah? She too struggled with anger that went beyond her control, which left the door open for the devil to freely operate in her life. She did not realize that she was contributing to her own demise by allowing anger to stay rooted in her life, but the result was significant damage nonetheless. She turned the anger she had toward her parents and ex-husbands against herself. She tried to commit suicide nine times. On the last attempt she succeeded at burning her house down and receiving third-degree burns all over her body.

When Sarah was finally ready for change in her life, she opened up the door, albeit just a crack, to the healing grace of the Savior. On her third visit to counseling with me, I (Larry) challenged her to reach out and touch someone with her life that week—just reach out to someone else. As you read earlier, there is something very powerful about touching the life of another person.

Sarah took that challenge and got a positive response, and not long after, she could be found going up and down the nine stories of the nursing home where she lived, talking to people and sharing life with them. Seeing her come to life, it was hard to imagine how Sarah had gotten to the point of complete and utter despair. How had she become so consumed with anger, bitterness and resentment that she was driven to take her own life?

Sarah had been married four times, and all her marriages had ended in divorce. She had felt rejection from all of her spouses, as well as her parents. These feelings of rejection first led to anger toward her parents and then toward her former husbands. At the age of 49, when she finally opened the door to counseling, she had saturated herself with repressed feelings of anger and had never been able to deal with, or appropriately express and understand, those destructive emotions. She was curious why I persisted in reaching out to her. "God loves you, Sarah, and so do I," I responded.

In the science fiction movie *The Matrix*, Keanu Reeves plays a character named Neo who explores the real world behind the computer-generated façade in which he had been living. Once he realizes he is living in a fake world, he meets Morpheus, a rebel leader who fights against the machines that created the Matrix, the computer fantasy that keeps most humans trapped. Morpheus is looking for the One, a messiah figure who will save the human world from extinction, as prophesied by the Oracle.

Morpheus believes that Neo is the One, but not everyone is convinced. At one point, one of Morpheus's crew tells Neo, "If you see an agent, you do what the rest of us do . . . *run*." Well, time and training continue, and as Neo grows in his faith, he has an encounter with one of these agents, a kind of super-policeman of the matrix. Instead of running away, however, he slowly turns around and, with confidence and a sense of divine authority, prepares for a fight. A sense of concern and panic comes over the team as they watch: "What's he doing? He should be trying to escape!"

Morpheus replies with an approving voice, "He's beginning to believe."

To believe in himself. To believe he is no longer a victim but a victor. To believe that he can change and that the world around him can be changed by him.

In much the same way, Sarah began to believe. She believed that if she could love herself, then possibly God could love her. She believed that there must be something out there for her. She began to see the miracle of having escaped nine suicide attempts, especially the last one. She began to believe that God had a purpose for her life.

The Word says, "And now these three remain: faith, hope and love. But the greatest of these is love" (1 Cor. 13:13) and "Faith is being sure of what we hope for and certain of what we do not see" (Heb. 11:1). If anger is the key to the door for Satan to bring despair, hopelessness and hatred of self and others, then an act of love is the key to opening doors of hope and belief that there is something far better for us and for those around us. There is hope promised to us from God (see Rom. 15:13). There is hope in Christ. There is hope in His grace. There is grace for tomorrow. This is a promise from the Bible: "'For I know the plans I have for you,' declares the LORD, 'plans to prosper you and not to harm you, plans to give you *hope* and a future'" (Jer. 29:11, emphasis added). There's that word again. *Hope.*

The word "hope" in this verse is an English translation of a Hebrew phrase that means "expected end" or "an arrival at that place or situation for which you longingly desire." Sarah, who is a Jew, was familiar with some of the Hebrew Scriptures. She began to see that God was personal, that Scripture prophesied of the coming Messiah and that Jesus fulfilled every prophecy concerning the Messiah (see Gen. 3:15; Num. 21:9; Ps. 110:4; Isa. 7:14-16; 9:1-7; 11:1-4; 42:1-4; 53:1-12).

After several months of searching out truth from the Old and New Testaments, Sarah received the ultimate grace of God when she received Jesus as her Lord and Savior. She arrived at the place she had longed for, even though she had not recognized her longing. She found *hope.*

She discovered that the anger, bitterness and resentment, which were the results of deep hurts in the past, could now be eliminated by the grace of Jesus. She realized that if she could be forgiven, she could forgive others through the power of Jesus' love and grace. She gave her parents, ex-husbands and children the same healing grace that God gave to her. In fact, the more people she was able to forgive, the more she was full of love, peace and His abundant life.

As she felt loved and accepted through Jesus, the negative emotions of anger, bitterness and resentment faded from Sarah's consciousness. Tracing the source of her anger, it was clear that the most important thing for her inner well-being was denied to her by the people who should have given her that love and acceptance. Only in Jesus Christ was she able to find healing grace, and once she did, the anger disappeared. Not only did the anger go away, but she was able to give unconditional love as she traveled up and down the convalescent nursing home touching and loving those around her. She had become an ambassador for Christ, spreading healing grace to hurting people like herself, and she began enjoying life for the first time in as long as she could remember.

The story gets better: The day Sarah moved out of the nursing home, there was a celebration of her life. Doctors, nurses, paramedics, aides and many patients gathered in the auditorium to hear her going-away speech. There was standing-room only and patients who were not ambulatory had their beds pushed into the halls outside the room. You could have heard a pin drop as she haltingly expressed her heart: "I used to be beautiful, but now I am ugly. I am becoming beautiful inside though I used to be ugly inside, full of anger and resentment and hatred. If I had to make a choice, I would choose being ugly outside and becoming beautiful inside. Jesus has made all the difference and Jesus will make a difference in your life."

There was not a dry eye in the auditorium. Her story sounds good, doesn't it? But it doesn't have to be just Sarah's story. When you make a decision to allow Jesus' grace to overcome you and His Word to dominate your thoughts, this kind of love can be your story, too. You have been in control long enough. It's time now for you to allow Christ to be in control.

You might be saying, "But I have an anger problem, not a problem with forgiveness." If you are honest and look into your heart, you will probably find someone in your past who has deeply hurt you and whom you have not forgiven. If you want to be relieved of the burden of anger and its consequences, you need to address the past and the people you need to forgive.

Don't let the sun go down on your anger. Just ask Bill. Just ask José. Just ask Sarah. Put Jesus in charge and He will lead you down the right path. What He did in Bill's, José's and Sarah's lives, He will do in yours. Take this moment to put the book down and to ask Jesus to fill your heart with the love you earnestly desire. Like Sarah, ask Jesus to help you understand that the unconditional love and acceptance we all need can only come from Him.

Forgive as You Have Been Forgiven

Imagine what our world would be like if everyone really lived out the following passage: "Get rid of all bitterness, rage and anger, brawling and slander along with every form of malice. Be kind and compassionate to one another, forgiving each other, just as in Christ God forgave you" (Eph. 4:31-32). This is *grace in action.* These verses tell us what to do: Put away anger and forgive; respond to others with grace.

So now that we know what we're supposed to do, the question is, *How?* Many have tried, yet when we try on our own, we fail. We can't do it ourselves—we need someone else in charge of our lives. And that person is Jesus. He is the one to ask for guidance, strength and the power to forgive.

Is it difficult to allow Jesus control of your life? For many it is, but remember Jesus' words: "Come to Me, all who are weary and are burdened and I will give you rest. Take My yoke upon you and learn from me, for I am gentle and humble in heart; and you will find rest for your souls. For My yoke is *easy,* and My burden is light" (Matt. 11:28-30, *NASB*, emphasis added). I don't know about you, but to me a yoke, something used to hold oxen in place, sounds as if it might be unmanageable. Yet Jesus says that His yoke is easy, that giving Him control is to our benefit. That's a relief!

In that close relationship of being "yoked" with Jesus comes not only knowledge of who He is, but also a direct connection to His power. That power enables us to do what we cannot do in our own strength. Jesus shares everything with us, including His relationship with the Father. His closeness to God can be our relationship with the Father (see John 14:6). Also included in His "everything" is grace, love, mercy, peace, true joy, and abundant, eternal and everlasting life (see John 17). Because of these things operating in us through the power of the Holy Spirit, healthy and loving relationships are available to us. We limit the blessing of healthy relationships when we try to do it in our own strength.

The initial invitation to experience relationship with Christ is a decision that results in a permanent bond to Christ. We become "sealed for the day of salvation" (Eph. 1:13; 4:30). It's important for us to understand the permanence of that decision. He will never leave nor forsake us. He will by no means ever cast us out. We become children of God when we surrender our lives to Him, and new creations when we receive His life. In addition, we become heirs of salvation and servants of the Lord (see Heb. 13:5; John 1:12; 6:37; 10:34; 1 John 5:11-13; 2 Cor. 5:17; Rom. 8:16-17; Gal. 2:20).

Lives being changed through Jesus are a beautiful thing to behold. If a picture is worth a thousand words, a life changed into the image of Christ is a library of grace! There is no other way to respond than with these three words: "Thank You, Lord!"

Sue's is a life that has been changed by the grace of God. She was one of three children who were severely emotionally, physically and verbally abused by their mother. Despite growing up and leaving home, the abuse continued. And despite suffering years of rejection, all three children sought their mother's love and acceptance all the more. Sue felt that she was especially disappointing to her mother. No matter how hard she tried, she could never gain her mother's approval. She just didn't measure up to her standards.

Finally, after living with more than 50 years of verbal and emotional abuse, Sue found the healing grace of the Lord Jesus, and that grace allowed her to forgive her mother—which was the turning point in Sue's healing. The anger, bitterness and outright hatred started to leave. The living nightmare of that hurtful relationship came to an end. Sue viewed herself and her mother in a new light: through eyes of grace. She could treat her mother with an attitude of grace and speak to her with a tongue of grace, because she had begun to operate out of a heart of grace through Jesus Christ.

Not only was Sue able to let go of the past emotions of hurt, rejection and anger, but also her mother began to change as she received grace from her daughter. When grace is engaged in a situation, the awesome power of God is released. Forgiveness plants a spiritual seed in a person who is forgiven. In the case of Sue and her family, the seed bloomed into a growing love relationship between Sue, her sister and their mother. Truly lives were transformed and changed more into the likeness of Jesus.

What had been hatred is now love.

What had been dissension is now peace.

What had been turmoil is now contentment.

What had been a bitter tongue is now made sweet.

What had been anger is replaced with forgiveness.

What had been brokenness is now wholeness.

Sue said, "I wasn't able to forgive my mother through my own ability or by just 'being religious'. . . I was only able to extend grace to my mother when I personally experienced grace through Jesus. Giving up myself to be crucified with Jesus made possible something I never could have done through myself" (see Eph. 2:8; Gal. 2:20).

Sue discovered that Jesus can and does make all the difference when He assumes His rightful place as Lord over our lives. He is and always will be Lord, and He deserves first place. All we need to do is to get ourselves out of the way by deferring our decisions, minds, wills and emotions to Him. It's true: We're required to be submissive and subordinate to His will and purposes for our lives—but the payoff is a life filled with grace and satisfaction.

How do those like Sue and others get rid of their anger? What can anyone do?

Resentment

I hear people in my office and in my seminars say to me again and again, "Norm, I don't want to be angry and let it out, especially to my family, but something just comes over me and I let it rip! There's a limit to what I can take. I know I really love others, but sometimes I cut them to pieces. I don't know what to do to change."

I usually respond with a question, "When you feel frustrated and angry with others, what do you focus on: How they react to what you said or how you would like them to act?"

They usually reply, "Oh, I keep mulling over what I didn't like and my destructive comments. I relive it again and again and beat up on myself for hurting them."

"Do you realize that by rehearsing your failures you are programming yourself to repeat them? And then you probably expect them not to change. Right?"

They usually respond with a puzzled look. But it's true. When you spend so much time thinking about what you *shouldn't* have done, you reinforce it. Furthermore, spending all your time and energy mentally rehashing your failures keeps you from formulating what you really *want* to do. Redirecting your time and energy toward a solution will make a big difference in how you communicate with anyone. Focus your attention on how you want to respond to your frustration and you *will* experience change!

Anger unresolved won't stay the same. It usually builds into resentment, that feeling of ill will toward another person. And it is usually accompanied by the desire to make the other person pay.

Think about this: When you hold resentment for another person, you have given him or her control of your emotional state. How do you feel about that? Most of us want to feel like we are in control of our own emotions—but you are not in control if you resent someone else! You have shifted the power source to that person. You're letting him or her push your emotional buttons of anger, frustration or bitterness.

When we fail to forgive, the plot of our life story swings toward tragedy or irony in light of the hurts caused by others. Our pain and disappointment seem to move us in one of two directions: *anger* or *denial.* Sometimes our bitterness grows deep and strong. We become firmly entrenched on a course of proving someone wrong or getting even.

In either case, we can become stuck in a life story that provides little meaning. Unforgiveness in the form of brazen or veiled hostility freezes a person into one frame of a life story. For the person stuck in unforgiveness, every act of the drama looks about the same.[3] But there's another way to consider what you're experiencing at that time.

Let's assume you're getting ready for a trip. You're looking forward to it. You bring out the new suitcase. You begin to select the items you want to take with you. The piles grow but you can stuff everything in the suitcase. Your suitcase begins to bulge and expand. Finally you get everything in and sit on it so that you can close the zipper. It doesn't have the same shape it used to, but that's all right. You try to lift it and you can barely budge it. You begin to drag it and that's the only way you'll get it to your car and ultimately to your destination. Already you're beginning to wonder if you need all this stuff and if it's worth the hassle. The trip is beginning to feel more like a burden than a pleasure.

This is the way it is for many who've been hurt by others. They wake up in the morning and fill a huge suitcase with all the memories of past hurts along with bitterness over anger, injustices, resentment and grudges. They itemize how others failed them and how they've failed themselves. It's not just baggage, but excess baggage. And it's not like they can ship this suitcase on ahead. It's handcuffed to them, so they drag it everywhere—it weighs them down, drains their energy and hinders their progress, all for things they don't even need.[4]

What are *you* carrying? A grudge, perhaps?

"Grudge" isn't a nice sounding word. It sits in your throat like a lump. A grudge comes when you've collected injustices that feed anger. It's like an emotional scab that's picked at for so long it becomes infected and the poison begins to move into every area of your life.

How do you know if you're carrying a grudge? There's an energy drain. It takes energy to remember hurts and keep score. It takes energy to rehearse what you'd like to say and to think of ways to punish the other person. It lets anger fester even to the point of rage. You know you're carrying a grudge when you look for ways to initiate payback. Another way to determine if grudges exist is to look at your physical and emotional health. There's physical fallout to grudges—stress, elevated blood pressure, ulcers, arthritis, and other ailments.

If you identify with any of these things, ask yourself, "Do I want to let go of my resentments or do I want revenge?" Many people struggle with letting the other person off the hook by forgiving him. With one foot on the road to forgiveness and the other on the road to revenge, you are immobilized. Why not make a commitment to forgive?

Giving up resentment may also involve giving up blame-shifting, feeling sorry for yourself, and/or talking negatively about the other person. Forgiveness costs. But the price tag of resentment demands continued payments (and with interest, at that!).

Steps to Give Up Resentment

The first four steps to give up resentment are a series that should be followed in sequence. Steps 6 and 7 are additional steps you should plan on including in your personal exercise of releasing anger.

1. Identify Your Feelings and Thoughts

Acknowledge the fact that you're angry. Call it what it is . . . anger. List on paper all the resentments, hurts and angry feelings you hold toward the other person. Describe in writing exactly what happened to you in as much detail as possible. State how you felt about it then and how you feel now.

Please be aware that you may experience considerable emotional upheaval as you make your list. Other old, previously buried feelings may surface at this time and you may feel upset for a while. As you think about and work on this list, ask God to reveal to you the deep, hidden pools of painful memories so your inner container of anger may be emptied. Thank Him that it's all right for you to wade through and expel these feelings at this time. Imagine Jesus Christ in the room with you saying, "I want you to be cleansed and free. You don't have to be emotionally lame, blind or deaf any longer."

Don't show your list to anyone. Releasing your anger at this point is not a face-to-face confrontation.

2. Set Your List Aside

After writing those things down, set your list aside and rest for a while. During this period of time, other feelings that did not appear on your first list might surface. You probably will not remember all your hurts, but you don't need to for this exercise to succeed.

3. Read Your List Aloud

Take your list into a room where there are two empty chairs facing each other. Sit in one of the chairs and imagine the other person sitting in the other. See the other welcoming you in a positive manner. Hear him saying something like, "I want to hear what you have to share with me. I will accept it. Please tell me what's on your heart. I need to hear it."

Look at the empty chair as though the other person is there. Take your time reading your list aloud to the imagined person. At first you may feel awkward or embarrassed about reading aloud in an empty room. But these feelings will pass. You may even find yourself amplifying what you have written as you share your list. Feel free to do so.

As you share, imagine that the other person is listening to you, nodding in acceptance and understanding your feelings. You may experience intense anger, depression, anxiety or other feelings as you continue with your list. Share these feelings with the imaginary person. Remember, Jesus Christ is there giving you permission to release your anger.

You may find that talking through only one of the feelings on your list makes you feel drained. It is important to stop and rest for a while. After some time of relaxation, resume your normal tasks for the day. Continue working through your list of feelings at another time.

4. Identify Your "Anger Thoughts"

Reword them to make them more accurate and positive. (The previous chapter can help you in this process). Ask yourself about each thought, "Is this reflecting the mind of Christ?"

5. Let Jesus Heal You

Before you conclude, close your eyes and visualize yourself, the other person and Jesus standing together with your hands on each other's shoulders. Spend several minutes visualizing this scene. At this point you may want to imagine that this person does not accept what you have said to them. This may be closer to reality than what you imagined earlier. But see yourself at peace, regardless of their acceptance.

6. Write a Letter

Another helpful method for releasing your anger is to write a letter to the person—a letter you will not send. This exercise is for your benefit, to help you verbalize your feelings.

It will be helpful for you to share your letter in the hearing of another person, such as a trusted friend. It should be someone who will listen and be supportive, and who will not make value judgments on you or your letter or violate your confidence. Sit across from your friend and read the letter aloud. Invite your friend to make comments, but only those that support you in what your letter intends. Be sure to thank him or her for listening.

7. Project a Positive Response

There is one more step that is a very important part of the healing process. After you release your negative emotions of anger and resentment, it's essential that you project a positive response such as love, acceptance or friendship toward others. If you don't replace the negative feelings with a positive response, you become emotionally neutral toward others. You become blasé—no feelings toward them at all. I've had a number of clients tell me that they feel nothing toward the other person. They have developed a state of emotional insulation, which means they have blocked off the expression of all feelings, and that's not healthy. Having released your anger and resentment, you must immediately begin responding toward others in a positive way.

The Power of Forgiveness

Chuck Colson tells about a woman who, during a graduation ceremony for inmates completing a Prison Fellowship program, rushed to the stage and wrapped her arms around a graduating inmate saying, "This young man is my adoptive son."

Everyone had tears in their eyes, for they knew this young man was behind bars for the murder of her daughter.

Remember that not forgiving means inflicting inner torment upon ourselves. Forgiveness is saying, "It's all right; it's over. I no longer resent you or see you as an enemy. I love you even if you cannot love me back."

Forgiveness is letting go of the intense emotions attached to incidents from our past. We still remember what happened, but we no longer feel intensely angry, frightened, bitter, resentful or damaged because of it. Forgiveness becomes an option once pain from the past stops dictating how we live our life today.

Forgiveness is recognizing that we no longer *need* our grudges and resentments, our hatred and self-pity. We do not need them as an excuse for getting less out of life than we want or deserve. Forgiveness is no longer wanting to punish the people who hurt us. It is no longer wanting to get even or have them suffer as much as we did. Forgiveness is freeing up and putting to better use the energy once consumed by holding grudges, harboring resentments and nursing unhealed wounds. Anger needs the experience of forgiveness to bring it to a close. Forgiveness is moving on.[5]

Lewis Smedes said, "When you forgive someone for hurting you, you perform spiritual surgery inside your soul; you cut away the wrong that was done to you so that you can see your 'enemy' through the magic eyes that can heal your soul. Detach that person from the hurt and let it go, the way children open their hands and let a trapped butterfly go free. Then invite the person back into your mind, fresh, as if a piece of history between you had been erased, its grip on your memory broken. Reverse the seemingly irreversible flow of pain within you."[6]

Forgiving Yourself

There is one other step you may not be expecting. You might need to forgive yourself. But why forgive yourself? There are several reasons. You might be blaming yourself and feeling guilty for:

- Not being able to change the person
- Not living up to others' expectations for you
- Not being loved and accepted by others
- Not being perfect in some way or every way
- Treating yourself the way others treated you (Can you identify how you have done this?)
- Mistreating yourself when you have difficult times as a result of your past
- Developing some of the same tendencies or problems you despise in others

Isn't it ironic that we often take out our frustrations on ourselves rather than on the person who hurt us? Perhaps we consider ourselves a safer target than the person we are struggling with. If another has hurt you in the past, you may feel that you can't vent your frustration on him because he'll only hurt you again. So you take the path of least resistance by shouldering the blame. This isn't necessary.[7]

We can choose to focus on ourselves as victims or as overcomers of difficulties.

We are able to forgive because God has forgiven us. He has given us a beautiful model of forgiveness. Allowing God's forgiveness to permeate our lives and renew us is the first step toward becoming a person of forgiveness. Consider praying this prayer of forgiveness:

Loving God, I praise You for Your wisdom, for Your love, for Your power. Thank You for life, with its joys and mysteries. Thank You for emotions—including anger.

Forgive me when I am led by my anger instead of being led by You. Make me aware of the things I do that produce anger in others—help me change those things. Show me how to clean up the offenses I commit toward others, and give me the courage to ask for forgiveness.

Help me to be able to look past the anger of another person and see Your creation in them, and to love them. Teach me how to forgive and give me the humility to forgive gracefully.

Arouse me to oppose injustice and other evils. Show me how to channel my energy that might otherwise be wasted in anger into constructive action in Your service.

You ask me to minister to persons around me. Help me understand what that means. Wake me up. Help me recognize that every moment of my life is an opportunity for Your love to flow through me.

Thank You, heavenly Father, for Your love. Thank You for sending Christ so that we might have life and have it to the full, and for sending the Holy Spirit to comfort and guide us through the uncertainties and confusion of everyday living.

In Christ's name. Amen.[8]

Free at Last

Judy and her husband, Carl, who was a dentist, came in for marriage counseling. They had problems that, regrettably, are common to many couples. She was unable to respond to her husband sexually. This was a sign of a deeper problem, which was her inability to really love him. Carl had gotten to a point where he was ready to terminate the marriage because of his continued frustration, yet his Christian faith had taught him divorce was an unacceptable option in this case.

"Seeking marriage counseling was the final straw; either the marriage and the sex got better or it was over," was his ultimatum.

She began to seek individual counseling for herself as well. She knew her inability to deal with trauma from her childhood caused by sexual molestation from her father probably was the cause of her current marriage difficulties. Judy faced the problem squarely and came to me (Larry) for assistance.

Like so many women who were sexually abused as children, she carried some anger, bitterness and resentment toward the perpetrator, in her case her father. Judy's mother, to her credit, divorced her husband when she found out about the incestuous abuse. The damage, however, had been done. Judy was traumatized by this violation.

When she became a Christian, her spirit was saved, but her soul (mind, will, emotions) was still captive to her abuser. As a result she had not seen or spoken to her father for about 20 years.

As discussed in the previous chapter about overcoming anger, it is the process of appropriating the grace of God through the conscious act of forgiveness that leads to healing and, eventually, to building a bridge of grace. When Judy was told that she needed to forgive her father in order for her to experience healing, she was determined to obey the conviction of the Holy Spirit that same day. She loved Jesus and she loved her husband, but she knew she had hated her father and that she had not extended to him that which she received from Jesus.

The process of putting her father in the chair, sharing all of her hurt, anger and bitterness and then releasing him from the debt toward her took several agonizing hours—but Judy pushed through, determined to be free through God's grace. Just as she finished the process, she received a call from her older brother, letting her know that their father was near death in the hospital and that he wanted to see her. She knew this set of events was sovereignly orchestrated by God to bring about healing for them both, so she immediately got on a plane and went to her dying father's bedside.

When she walked into the room, he rose up in the bed and extended his arms to her, as if rising from a grave of his own creation. She embraced him as a child embraces a father after a long absence, and they cried together in each other's arms. After what seemed like an eternity, her father was the first to speak.

"Please forgive me," he said through the tears.

"I already have, Dad," were Judy's words as her father breathed his last.

Instead of carrying the weight of anger and bitterness, she was so grateful that she had a chance to forgive him before he died.

"Larry, no words can tell you how much that meant to me and how it has opened me up emotionally and sexually with my husband," she later shared.

God is good and wants us all to experience abundant life through Christ. Grace is a gift for us and others if we will only put Jesus in charge and listen to His voice, just as Judy listened to the voice of the Holy Spirit. God's grace not only saves us from our sin but that same grace heals us of our past wounds, hurts and rejections.

I really believe that no one can let go of something as devastating as what Judy went through as a child without fully appropriating God's grace. Otherwise, all the pain and suffering that has been stored in the recesses of the mind will continue to haunt and control us in a sick and debilitating way. The greater the injury to the soul, the more grace is needed.

Putting Jesus in charge, by allowing Him to take control and speak to the hurt and pain, is possible if we are willing to forgive those who have hurt us. Without true forgiveness, there can be no restoration. Holding on to pain and rejection gives Satan a right to reside within that situation and continue to torment us, yet we are set free if we remember and live according to the truth: All of the pain and rejection has already been paid for on the cross. We do not have to hold on to it anymore. You and I are the only ones who will be hurt if we cannot release it. We, like Judy, can say:

"*Free*. I'm *free*. Thank God, I'm *free* at last."

CHAPTER 7

Communicating Grace

W e were created for relationships, not to live in isolation or in disconnection from one another. We were created to be connected to God and to one another.

What connects us to one another? *Our words.* What disconnects us from God and from others? *Our words.* Proverbs says, "Pleasant words are as a honeycomb, sweet to the mind and healing to the body" (16:24, *AMP*) and "Death and life are in the power of the tongue, and they who indulge it shall eat the fruit of it [for death or life]" (18:21, *AMP*). There is power in our words that can build up or tear down.

Alaska, 1988. Prince William Sound. The *Exxon Valdez.* Remember that name? These words remind us of one of our country's worst environmental disasters. The giant oil tanker spilled 11 million gallons of crude oil into the Sound, contaminating more than 1,200 miles of shoreline. The spill was responsible for the deaths of 1,000 sea otters and more than 100,000 birds, including 150 bald eagles. Losses to the fishing industry exceeded $100 billion. The aftermath of the oil spill will be with us for years.

Contamination has occurred in our cities as well. Toxic materials thoughtlessly dumped into landfills years ago are coming back to haunt us. Toxic fumes are now seeping into homes constructed over these landfills, and entire communities have been evacuated because of the dangers of toxicity.

On an international scale, super-powers continue to argue about the stockpile of nuclear weapons posing imminent danger to the entire world. Some weapons are being dismantled and destroyed while others are being unilaterally reduced in number—while still others are being produced.

Just as our world has problems with contamination, toxicity and weapons, so too do our homes—even Christian homes. We often poison and wound each other with the words we use. You may have grown up with parents who used words as weapons, and you hoped you wouldn't do the same. But it's a challenge not to repeat the pattern in some way. Through Christ, however, you can become the transition person to break the cycle and develop healthy communication skills, those that reflect the presence of Jesus Christ and the grace you've been given. Such a change is possible!

Toxic Verbal Weapons

I call them "toxic weapons"—those cruel, caustic, bitter, degrading and judgmental words we use to hurt one another. They contaminate, wound, poison and destroy others emotionally. Our words are often launched as verbal missiles to attack behavior, appearance, intelligence, competence or value as a person.

Words bruise and batter on the inside like physical blows bruise and lacerate the skin. That's why we call it verbal *abuse*. We're often unaware of the damage our words cause because we can't see the inner cuts and bruises. Even when the verbal assault stops, the emotional damage continues within the person. Think back to your childhood: Were toxic verbal weapons used in your home? Do you still carry the inner scars from hurtful words launched at you by your parents, brothers, sisters or friends?

Some forms of verbal abuse are more subtle, but they hurt just as much. This indirect abuse manifests as sarcasm, teasing and subtle putdowns veiled in humor.

One of the more common—and not so subtle—toxic verbal weapons found in our arsenal are *words of judgment.* When the guns of judgment are fired, the target ends up overloaded with blame, making him feel unacceptable to you and himself.

Belittling is one of the most damaging forms of judgment. To belittle someone is to make light of his behavior, feelings, thoughts or accomplishments.

Blaming is another. I've seen people use this approach to avoid accepting responsibility for their own actions. They blame another for "causing" their problems or emotional upsets. You've probably heard yourself or others say, "You make me so upset." "Your behavior is going to be the death of me." "I wish you wouldn't make me so angry." What they are actually saying is, "This wouldn't have happened if it hadn't been for you." And how do you think the other will respond? You're right—defensively!

Dan was desperate to save his blended family. He had a child from a previous marriage, and his current wife, Lucy, had three children from her previous marriage. Dan's daughter, Laura (17), and Lucy's daughter Shelly (15) were still living at home. Lucy's two oldest daughters were in college.

Lucy was the dominant spouse of the two. She accused her husband of being partial to his daughter, Laura, and was convinced that Laura thought she loved her daughter, Shelly, more than she loved her. Furthermore, there was considerable strain between Lucy and her Laura. Laura felt belittled by her stepmother for every incident or argument that occurred between her and Shelly.

When the family began counseling, they discovered that the way they communicated did not help their relationship, but widened the gap between them. They either used small talk or tried to change others by resorting to a few of what we call the "dirty dozen." These are responses that push others away rather than draw them closer: complaining, criticizing, judging, being negative, blaming, labeling, becoming defensive, ignoring, assuming without checking, misusing authority, seducing or creating guilt within the other person.

It amazed Lucy and Laura to see how much their conversation reflected these two styles of communication. Almost 95 percent of their verbal communication was damaging in these ways.

Dan and Lucy finally recognized what had happened in their family: The negative interaction between Lucy and Laura finally resulted in Laura rebelling. That rebellion took the negative interactions to the next level: When both the parent and child begin to use the "dirty dozen," the result was intensified arguing, fighting and yelling. This type of communication never resolves conflicts or issues, but rather turns the conflict combative. This could eventually reach a point of hostility in which one spouse or child leaves or lashes out physically.

Satan really goes to work to distance you from God and from others when you act in a demanding way. His desire is to kill your love for God and others. Left unchecked, this can lead to isolation, separation or divorce, alienating you from your loved ones. It is Satan's way of destroying your marriage, family and other relationships.

But when God the Father, Son and Holy Spirit really go to work, interacting in a positive, healthy way is possible. God desires to save marriages, families and friendships.

Dan and Lucy began to employ a positive style of interaction (see styles 3 and 4 on the Four Styles of Communication

Chart at the end of this chapter). They moved away from demanding of one another to adjusting and listening. They built a bridge of grace together as they forgave each other as well as their previous spouses. Soon the two daughters, Laura and Shelly, also learned how they could better relate to one another in a healthy way. They eliminated the "dirty dozen" and replaced them with positive ways of talking, including using the six relationship healing phrases. Even the two older children in college noticed the difference and sought to be more connected.

"What a difference Jesus and grace makes in a family," said Dan. "It's like we were dying as a family but now we are alive and learning to communicate and relate to one another in ways of love and forgiveness. God's grace is really sufficient."

Fault-Finding

One of the most destructive forms of verbal abuse is *fault-finding*. It's another form of blame and judgment. You can't express God's grace to others by blame. The fault-finding person seems to have an insatiable need to point out the defects of others. He's always looking at another person through a critical lens and pointing out what she did or didn't do, what she said or didn't say, and what she might or might not do in the future. Even the most insignificant errors or defects are quickly exposed and corrected. Those who are challenged about their fault-finding often respond defensively: "I'm just trying to help her." But the pain that the person experiences from consistent criticism and correction often outweighs the benefits.

Frequently a fault-finding person is a perfectionist who holds the unrealistic expectation that he and others ought to be perfect. This expectation is the trigger for verbal attacks and pressure when the other fails. Unfortunately, the other person becomes the scapegoat for the fault-finder's own failure to be perfect, and because she can't live up to his standard of perfection, she often becomes a procrastinator. Her fear of failing to do things perfectly prompts her to postpone the actions for which she fears she will be criticized. The more she procrastinates, the more overwhelmed she feels by the pressure to perform. Soon she's immobilized by her lack of perfection and gives up.

Fault-finding isn't always verbal. A sneering look, a frown or a condemning gesture also convey displeasure. Nonverbal put-downs are often difficult to interpret, and leave you wondering, "What's going on? Am I crazy or are you?" Silence is a classic form of control, punishment and criticism in a dysfunctional home. God did not put us into families to be silent. We were created to communicate with each other, but in a healthy way, which reflects Jesus' presence in our lives.

Here are several reasons why fault-finding is so destructive in a relationship:

• Fault-finding deeply wounds. Constant verbal and nonverbal criticism says, "I don't accept you for who you are at this time in your life. You don't measure up, and I can't accept you until you do." In more than 40 years of counseling, I have heard multitudes of people in my office cry out in pain, "My parents' criticism ripped me apart as a child. They made me feel like dirt. I never felt accepted, and I'm still looking for someone who will tell me I'm alright."

• Fault-finding also wounds the one speaking. The wounded person becomes afraid or angry and retaliates through overt or covert withdrawal, resentment and aggression.

• Fault-finding really won't change anyone. Though the person may appear to change her behavior in response to criticism, her heart rarely changes.

• Fault-finding is contagious. A fault-finding person teaches intolerance to others by example. Thus those influenced (such as the fault-finder's children) learn to be critical of themselves and others.

• Fault-finding accentuates negative traits and behaviors. When you pay undue attention to a person's mistakes or irresponsible behaviors, you tend to reinforce them instead of eliminate them.

Helen went through a very painful, devastating divorce. Her husband left her to live with her best friend, leaving Helen with two painful rejections at the same time. Needless to say, she was extremely depressed. As with many individuals in similar circumstances of infidelity and divorce, she thought she would never marry again. After two years, however, she started dating a man. Unfortunately, he left her as well. Within a few months of that rejection, she went through another broken relationship.

Helen then met a "nice guy" named Ben who was crazy about her, but she was less than passionately in love with him. She married him despite her lack of strong emotional attachment because she had finally found a man who highly esteemed her.

After a few months, Helen began to find fault with Ben. Though she tried to deal with it on her own, she didn't succeed. It was evident that she still had a lot of unresolved anger that needed to be addressed. Although on the surface she felt she had forgiven her ex-husband and friend, in reality she hadn't. Instead, she had opted for a pseudo-intellectual forgiveness: As a Christian she knew she could not tolerate unforgiveness in her life, but she had not dealt emotionally with the anger.

Ultimately, Helen's nagging at and fault-finding with Ben resulted in divorce. She felt she deserved more and was determined to find another man about whom she could feel passionate. Not only had she been unable to give unconditionally to Ben, but she also hadn't received what she desired emotionally from him either.

For his part, Ben had a difficult time letting go of his relationship with Helen. He too had been married before and now he was facing a second rejection. He struggled, because rejection is one of the most difficult experiences from which to recover. It hurts to hear, "I don't want you."

Though repetitive fault-finding is hazardous to relationships, there are times when we need to give constructive guidance. But how you express that corrective guidance makes all the difference in the world to how another receives it! Negative, fault-finding condemnation doesn't promote a person's inner growth.

Furthermore, condemnation isn't scriptural. Jesus said, "Do not judge and criticize and condemn others, so that you may not be judged and criticized and condemned yourselves . . .

In accordance with the measure you deal out to others it will be dealt out again to you" (Matt. 7:1-2, *AMP*). Paul wrote, "Let us no more criticize and blame and pass judgment on one another, but rather decide and endeavor never to put a stumbling block or an obstacle or a hindrance in the way of a brother" (Rom. 14:13, *AMP*).

Criticism

Criticism is the initial negative response that opens the door for other destructive responses to follow. Criticism is different from complaint because it attacks a person's personality and character, usually with blame. Most criticism is over-generalized ("You always . . .") and personally accusing (the word "you" is central and the word "should" is given prominence).[1]

Criticism is usually destructive, even though critics say they're just trying to remold their partner or child into better people by offering some constructive advice. But too often, criticism doesn't construct; it demolishes. It doesn't nourish a relationship; it poisons it. Criticism accuses, tries to make others feel guilty, intimidates and is often an outgrowth of personal resentment.

Criticism comes in many shapes and sizes. You've heard of "zingers," those lethal, verbal missiles. A zinger comes at you with a sharp point and a dull barb that catches the flesh as it goes in. The power of these sharp, caustic statements is seen when you realize that one zinger can undo 20 acts of kindness. Men in particular don't handle being on the receiving end of these very well.

Once a zinger lands, the effect is similar to a radioactive cloud that settles on an area of what used to be prime farmland. The land is so contaminated by the radioactivity that any seeds that are scattered fail to take root, die out and are washed away by the elements. It takes decades for the contamination to dissipate. Kind acts and loving words, following a radioactive zinger, find a similar hostile soil. It may take a long time before there is a receptivity or positive response to positive overtures.

Lola came from a critical, belittling family that was always arguing, fault-finding, yelling, fighting and sending a multitude of zingers to each other, creating unhappiness and family chaos. The anger, bitterness, hostility and unforgiveness were very apparent. Lola learned and developed anger from repeated confrontations, just as the Bible predicts happens when parents create a home full of criticism. Ephesians 6:4 in *The Living Bible* paraphrase states:

And now a word to you parents. Don't keep on scolding and nagging your children, making them angry and resentful. Rather, bring them up with the loving discipline the Lord himself approves, with suggestions and godly advice.

Children learn what they live! Dysfunction and abuse result when negativity is a family's norm in communication. A constant diet of negativity has a devastating effect on marriage and children. It can become a generational pattern or curse.

Lola wanted to break her family pattern of criticism, blame and zingers with her husband and children. She called one day and said, "Larry, the Holy Spirit has convicted me that I must forgive my father and mother if I am ever going to break this generational curse [pattern]." She had traced this angry pattern all the way back to her great-grandfather. She resolutely decided that she must forgive her mother and father as Christ had forgiven her (see Eph. 4:32). She discovered that she could give that grace to her parents. Lola wanted to be free and not continually spinning her wheels in anger, bitterness and unforgiveness. In other words, she wanted to be set free—and she was! You too can be set free to be all Jesus wants you to be, and experience what grace can do to heal your relationships and the wounds of the past.

Zingers are devastating for relationships. They can wipe out all the sunshine. You can have a wonderful day being kind, thoughtful and tender for hours, but then, in a moment of anger, you open your mouth with a put-down. It's as though a giant eraser came sweeping through your relationship and wiped out all your positive actions and words. This principle is similar to the fact that it takes 20 minutes of exercise to work off a candy bar, but only one minute to eat another one and invalidate all the good effects of your exercise.

Defensiveness

Being constantly on the receiving end of criticism, fault-finding and zingers causes us to erect walls. It's understandable. We want to protect ourselves, so we hide behind a wall that pushes others away. This wall is called *defensiveness*.

"I didn't do that; you just think I did."

"You're the one who never listens . . . don't point a finger at me."

Defensiveness has many forms and flavors. No matter what your spouse says, you deny it or insist you're not the one to blame. Or you make excuses: "The dog ate the list you gave me." Or you manifest a defensive attitude in your body language.

You can view your spouse's words (complaints or concerns) either as an attack or as information that is strongly expressed. The choice is yours. But if you're following the Bible as your guide for communication, hear this: You need to admit when you're wrong. Most of the time, defensiveness isn't necessary.

A lot of people find it difficult if not impossible to say, "I'm wrong; you may be right." If necessary, practice saying this sentence so that you will be able to say it when it fits a disagreement or discussion with your spouse. When you honestly own up to knowing that you are wrong and the other person is right, you improve communication a thousand-fold and deepen your relationship with your spouse, children and others. The apostle James tells us to admit our faults to one another and to pray for each other (see Jas. 5:16). Proverbs 28:13 also has good advice: "A man who refuses to admit his mistakes can never be successful. But if he confesses and forsakes them, he gets another chance" (TLB).

Sometimes you will have to admit you are wrong in the face of your spouse's criticism, and this is never easy. It also can be tricky. Be sure not to play the "I know it's all my fault" game with your mate. It's easy to use that line to manipulate your mate into feeling apologetic and taking some of the blame, even when they are not at fault: "Well, I suppose it's partially my fault, too."

When you face your spouse's criticism and know it's correct, keep these proverbs in mind:

If you refuse criticism you will end in poverty and disgrace, if you accept criticism you are on the road to fame (Prov. 13:18, *TLB*).

Don't refuse to accept criticism; get all the help you can (Prov. 23:12, *TLB*).

It is a badge of honor to accept valid criticism (Prov. 25:12, *TLB*).

If you're really at fault, be willing to admit it. Say something like, "You know, I do think I'm to blame here. I'm sorry for what I said and I'm sorry that I hurt you. What can I do to help or make up for it?" These phrases do wonders.

Quarreling

What is causing the quarrels and fights among you? Isn't it because there is a whole army of evil desires within you? You want what you don't have, so you kill to get it. You long for what others have, and can't afford it, so you start a fight to take it away from them. And yet the reason you don't have what you want is that you don't ask God for it. And even when you do ask you don't get it because your whole aim is wrong—you want only what will give *you* pleasure (Jas. 4:1-3, *TLB*).

Does this Scripture mean that we're not going to have conflicts at all? No. Very few dissimilar individuals in families can spend time together without conflict—individual tastes, preferences, habits, likes and dislikes, personality differences, values and standards confront each other at some point. Remember, however, that conflict and disagreement are not the same as quarreling.

Verbal conflict in itself is not harmful; it can open doors of communication. On the other hand, a quarrel or a verbal conflict in which the emotions have taken over closes the doors of communication, because resolving the conflict is no longer the main objective—defeating, hurting or making sure the other person loses is. When the quarrel is over, there is usually a greater distance between the people or a residual bad feeling. The Word of God is specific about what to do with quarrels:

People without good sense find fault with their neighbors, but those with understanding keep quiet (Prov. 11:12, *NCV*).

Starting a quarrel is like a leak in a dam, so stop it before a fight breaks out (Prov. 17:14, *NCV*).

Foolish people are always fighting, but avoiding quarrels will bring you honor (Prov. 20:3, *NCV*).

Just as charcoal and wood keep a fire going, a quarrelsome person keeps an argument going (Prov. 26:21, *NCV*).

If it is possible, as far as it depends on you, live at peace with everyone (Rom. 12:18, *NIV*).

Make every effort to live in peace with all men and to be holy; without holiness no one will see the Lord (Heb. 12:14).

We must remember that we have the power to change another's life by what we say. Paul said we need to watch our words: "When you talk do not say harmful things, but say what people need—words that will help others become stronger" (Eph. 4:29, *NCV*).

How Do I Change?

Perhaps you're thinking, *All right, Norm. You've made your point. But I still get frustrated with others. How do I change my communication responses from verbal abuse to helpful and encouraging words?*

By asking for help, you've taken the first step. Before you can make any changes, you've got to acknowledge your need to change. Congratulations—you're on your way!

The second step is to clearly identify the destructive verbal patterns you're employing. To help you do so, I suggest that you do what I've asked numerous individuals in my counseling office to do: Begin recording your conversations at home. Get a cassette recorder and several blank 90-minute tapes. Turn the recorder on at mealtimes, at the onset of a family argument or at other occasions when the family is together, and let it run. After a few self-conscious moments, everyone will forget about the recorder and begin to interact normally.

After you have recorded several interactions, listen to the tapes. As you listen, focus on your own communication patterns instead of judging others for theirs. Write down your abusive comments from the tape and summarize the kinds of verbal weapons you use (sarcasm, teasing, fault-finding, blaming, belittling, and so on).

The third step is to begin integrating the guidance of Scripture into your communication. *You need to line up with the Word of God.* Here's a practical way to do so:

- Write out each of the following verses about communication from Proverbs on a separate index card: 10:19; 12:18; 14:29; 16:24; 17:9; 19:11; 29:20.

- On the back of each card, write a statement describing how you see yourself complying with that verse. Make it specific and personal, perhaps beginning with the words "I will . . ."

- Carry the cards with you for the next 30 days, and read each verse and statement aloud several times a day. By the end of 30 days, you will have probably memorized most of the verses and begun to integrate their concepts into your communication.

I've discovered that it's helpful to involve your spouse or a trusted friend in this process. Tell somebody what you're doing, read him or her the statements you've written and ask that person to hold you accountable to follow through with the exercise.

I also suggest that you keep a personal "communication growth" diary. Write down your progress in attitudes, feelings and communication daily. All entries must be positive; don't keep score of the problems or defeats. Note how you change and how others respond to your changes. Share your responses with your spouse or friend. At the end of each week, reread the entire diary from the beginning. Keep your diary faithfully for one month, and then decide if you want to continue for another month.

Communicating Grace in Marriage

Let's take this one step further and talk about communication in marriage. In marriage many couples communicate as though life is a contest. They challenge each other, compete and continually resist each other. In our society we are taught to be competitive. We believe there are winners and losers, and it is best to be a winner (at all costs). There are many winners, however, who have won the battles but lost the war.

A great way to handle another person's point of view is not to fight it but to try to find some point of agreement with it. This allows you to move along *with* the person instead of confronting him head on. The attitude needed is, "How can we both achieve some of what we want?" Life is *not* a contest! But often husbands and wives make it one!

I also recommend that couples (or any two people in a relationship) regularly give words of affirmation to each other. Look for the positive changes in the other person and tell them about it along with a hug or kiss. Let them know you really notice the positive change and how much you appreciate it. This brings forth positive reinforcement that promotes a better relationship.

When you employ toxic verbal weapons in your communication, you're standing against a person. But when your words are full of nurture and encouragement, you're standing with him. First Thessalonians 5:11 states, "Therefore encourage one another and build each other up, just as in fact you are doing."

Called to Encourage

A child needs his parents to believe in his potential. A spouse needs the other to believe in his or her potential. Believe in others. Focus on their strengths to build their self-esteem, self-confidence and feelings of worth. Help others see how God views them. Become a talent scout, helping others discover their uniqueness, giftedness and potential. We're called to be encouragers.

Scripture states that others will know that we are Christians by the love we show one another. And one of the ways we reflect this love is by being an encourager. Look at what God's Word tells us to do.

In Acts 18:27, the word "encourage" means "to urge forward or persuade." In 1 Thessalonians 5:11, it means "to stimulate another person to the ordinary duties of life." How can you do this in what you say?

Consider 1 Thessalonians 5:14: "And we earnestly beseech you, brethren, admonish (warn and seriously advise) those who are out of line—the loafers, the disorderly and the unruly;

encourage the timid and fainthearted, help and give your support to the weak souls [and] be very patient with everybody—always keeping your temper."

Scripture uses a variety of words to describe both our involvement with others as well as the actual relationship. "Urge" (*parakaleo*) means "to beseech or exhort." It is intended to create an environment of urgency to listen and respond to a directive. It's a mildly active verb. Paul uses it in Romans 12:1 and in 1 Corinthians 1:4. How could you do this in what you say?

The word translated "encourage" (*paramutheomai*) means "to console, comfort and cheer up." This process includes elements of understanding, redirecting of thoughts, and a general shifting of focus from the negative to the positive. In the context of the verse, it refers to the timid ("fainthearted," *KJV*) individual who is discouraged and ready to give up. It's a matter of lending your faith and hope to the person until his own develops. How could you do this in what you say?

"Help" (*anechomai*) primarily contains the idea of "taking interest in, being devoted to, rendering assistance, or holding up spiritually and emotionally." It is not so much an active involvement as a positive approach. It suggests the idea of coming alongside a person and supporting her. In the context of 1 Thessalonians 5:14, it seems to refer to those who are incapable of helping themselves. How could you do this in what you say?

First Thessalonians 5:11 says, "Therefore encourage one another and build each other up, just as in fact you are doing."

Hebrews 3:13 says we're to "encourage one another every day." In the setting of this verse, encouragement is associated with protecting the believer from callousness.

Hebrews 10:25 says, "Let us encourage one another." This time the word means to keep someone on their feet who, if left to himself, would collapse. Your encouragement serves like the concrete pilings of a structural support. How could you do this in what you say?

One of my favorite verses is Proverbs 12:25: "A person's anxiety will weigh him down, but an encouraging word makes him joyful" (GOD'S WORD).

Affirming and encouraging responses can literally change our lives because we want and need others to believe in us. An unusual example of this affirmation is found in the Babemba tribe in southern Africa. When one of the tribal members has acted irresponsibly, he or she is taken to the center of the village. Everyone in the village stops work and gathers in a large circle around the person. In turn, each person, regardless of age, speaks to the person and recounts the good things he or she has done. All the positive incidents in the person's life, plus the good attributes, strengths and kindnesses, are recalled with accuracy and detail. Not one word about the problem behavior is even mentioned.

This ceremony, which sometimes lasts for several days, isn't complete until every positive thing has been spoken by those assembled. The person in the circle is literally flooded with affirmation and then is welcomed back into the tribe. Can you imagine how the person feels about himself or herself after this? Can you imagine his or her desire to continue to reflect those positive qualities? Perhaps a variation of this ceremony is needed in marriages and families today.[2]

The Word of God is very clear about what we're to do. To be a consistent encourager, you will need to reflect the character qualities of 1 Corinthians 13. Here they are amplified in a unique way:

- Patient (tolerant of frailties, imperfections and short-comings of the people in your life)
- Kind (tender, thoughtful toward others)
- Not jealous (of genuine friendships with others or of the special gifts and talents of others)
- Not boastful (about personal appearance or achievements in an attempt to compete with another)
- Not arrogant (not disdainful of others' looks or achievements; don't belittle anyone)
- Not rude (not inconsiderate of others' needs or feelings)
- Not insistent on your own way (willing to compromise, to consider another's needs and interests)
- Not irritable (don't snap at others; approachable)
- Not resentful (don't hold grudges; forgiving)
- Don't rejoice in wrong (don't delight in others' misfortunes; don't keep score or tally perceived wrongs)
- Rejoice in right (truthful; don't try to conceal things from others)
- Bear all things (support others in times of struggle)
- Believe all things (don't challenge words of others)
- Hope all things (don't wallow in pessimism about your relationship; keep a positive attitude)

• Endure all things (don't give in to pressures of life; willing to stand by others when they're having personal struggles)

Pray!

Another essential element for true change in the way we communicate (that's often overlooked because it seems so obvious) is prayer. We must communicate openly and honestly with God on a regular basis if we're going to receive the grace, faith, wisdom and strength to change.

Consider the story of a former military family. This once-close, Christian family of eight had been through a lot together. The mother, Emily, was distraught over her daughter, Becky, who had been diagnosed with cancer. Emily and her husband, Charley, went to Becky's home in another state to help care for her and the grandchildren. Emily wanted to do more for her daughter, but the fact that Becky didn't want her children to know she had cancer became increasingly difficult for Emily to deal with. After three sleepless nights, she thought perhaps some wine would help settle her nerves so that she could better handle the situation.

Unfortunately, this made matters worse. Becky discovered Emily drinking, and she became very upset. She jumped to the conclusion that her mother was an alcoholic and asked her parents to leave.

Charley and Emily tried to explain that that wasn't the case but Becky wouldn't listen—she insisted they leave immediately. When they got back home, Emily was so depressed she had to be hospitalized to receive anti-anxiety and anti-depressant medication. Still, she and Charley attempted to reach out to their daughter. Becky, however, wouldn't talk to them. She even sent back gifts that they had sent to their grandchildren.

Becky shared with one of her brothers, Ben, what she thought had occurred, explaining her perception that their mom was an alcoholic. She told him that their parents deserted her in her time of greatest need. Ben believed Becky and he, too, became angry at Emily and Charley. Ben wouldn't listen to his parent's explanation. He thought they were just making up excuses for their actions in abandoning Becky.

Not only would Becky not listen to her mom and dad, but she also brought other siblings into the conflict. Half of the children allied themselves *with* Mom and Dad and the other half alienated themselves *from* Mom and Dad. Could grace bring healing to this family? Could they forgive and be reconciled to each other? All the misunderstanding and assumptions taking place in this family highlight the necessity of healthy communication.

There is no such thing as perfect parents or perfect children. Bridges of grace need to be built in marriages, families and other relationships so that issues, problems, hurts, rejections and mis-understandings can be resolved and healed. This family allowed issues of the past to break down their relationships. Because these issues hadn't been talked out and dealt with over the years, there was more tension and strife rather than healthy, loving interaction.

Emily and Charley have intensified their prayers. They have reached out in every way possible to reconcile their family. They are determined to extend grace to all their children in hopes that they will extend grace back to them and each other. They believe that there isn't room for hatred in the kingdom of God, nor in their family, and their daily prayer is: "God, grant our family favor through Your grace. Bring about repentance, forgiveness, reconciliation and restoration to our family. Let this lead more fully to the knowledge of the way, truth and life, Jesus Christ. Let our family come to our senses and escape the snare of the devil as we have been held captive by him much too long" (paraphrase from 2 Tim. 2:25-28). These parents believe that God will strengthen them to continue reaching out and have the patience to never give up.

Hopefully, through Jesus, Emily and Charley's alienated children will exercise grace to be reconciled to God and to those they've wounded. There will be healing when they're able to express the six relationship grace phrases. Can you imagine the response when this family can say to one another, "You were right," "I was wrong," "I am sorry," "Please forgive me," "I forgive you" and "I love you"?

Let's recap the steps to *communicating grace* in our relationships:

1. *Acknowledge your need for change and seek help.* It's likely that you've already taken this step, but take a minute to tell the Lord what you want to change. Write down the name of a person—a trusted friend, family member, pastor or counselor—with whom you can share this.

2. *Clearly identify the destructive verbal patterns or communication that you want to change.* A great thing to do now

would be to write down *specifically* what you want to change about the way you communicate (for example, to be an encourager rather than a criticizer, to notice the good in people rather than the bad, to be able to communicate frustration and anger in a kind, controlled manner). If you have a tape-recorder, record your conversations, listen to them and write down your observations as described above.

3. *Meditate on Scripture.* Follow the instructions above for writing out verses that deal with speech and communication. Use the verses above, but also take time to do your own search of Scripture. Write the verses you find, along with your personal commitment statement on the back. Put them somewhere you'll read them often and take time each day to chew on them, praying that the Lord will make them a reality in your life.

4. *Begin your communication growth journal,* as described above.

5. *Make the effort to acknowledge and affirm the other person's point of view (even if it's different from your own).* You might not totally agree with what the person says or believes, but you can foster good communication by listening and withholding judgment (even in your mind!) of his or her perspective. This is truly walking in grace!

6. *Encourage!* Make the most of every opportunity to encourage your spouse, child, parent, friends, co-workers and everyone you interact with. Note their positive attributes and let them know what you love about them.

7. *Pray!* True change in any aspect of our lives only comes through vibrant relationship with the Lord. Continue to take your communication challenges to Him and ask Him daily to make you a minister of His healing grace.

By God's grace, you can appropriate the above in your life through Jesus Christ. Your life and your relationships will be greatly improved. Healing grace can take place within you and your relationships, as you will see in the next chapter.

DIAGRAM III

Four Styles of Communication

Style	Intention	Behavior	Characteristics, Voice and Body
I	Friendly Sociable Playful	Small talk Data Weather	No one counts Voice: unexpressive Body: non-threatening Non-risky Little/no self-disclosure Don't rock the boat, placating
II	Forcing change	Complaining Ignoring Critical Unchecked assumptions Judging Authoritative Negative Sueductive Blaming Creating guilt within other person Labeling Defensive	I count—emotionally charged Voice: firm, whiny, angry, loud, harsh Body: striking out, threatening Closed communication No self-disclosure
III	To understand and explore: past, present, future	Supportive Explanations Posing solutions and alternatives Checking out assumptions Making an impression	Qualified: I count, you count Voice: calm, quiet, hesitant Body: more receptive Opening up communication Some self-disclosure
IV	"In-touch Awareness"	Edifying (Eph. 4:29) Minister grace (Eph. 4:29) Lift up, not tear down Deal with issues openly Loving (1 Cor. 13:1, John 4:16) Submitting unto one another (Eph. 5:21) Accepting (Luke 10:27; Eph. 5:25) Empathetic Trusting and revealing Understanding Focus on now—forget the past (Phil. 3:13) Contributing Forgiving (Eph. 4.31-32)	You count as much as I count Voice: dialogue— harmonious, open, pleasant, frank Body: giving and receptive Open/free communication Spontaneous self-disclosure Value self and others Take charge of own life (with God's help) Awareness of others' skills, needs

CHAPTER 8

The Secret of the Universe

L uke 6:38 says, "Give, and it will be given to you; good measure, pressed down, shaken together, running over, they will pour into your lap. For by your standard of measure it will be measured to you in return" (*NASB*).

This is called *the secret of the universe*—the ability to *give* and to *receive*.

The human body breathes in and breathes out. The ocean tide comes in and goes out. Plants take in carbon dioxide and give out oxygen. When you think about it, all of life is giving and receiving (see diagrams IV and V).

Give Out, Receive In

A physicist named Adam came to the office for counseling, and after listening to his problems, I presented the concept of "give out, receive in" to him. His response was immediate and dramatic. Later he exclaimed, "It was like a light bulb came on in my head."

Up to this point, Adam knew something was wrong in his life, but he didn't know how to fix it. He certainly was receiving in life but he was doing very little giving back—not much beyond his paycheck to his family. As we talked, he reflected on physics, a subject he knew well. He talked about how everything that seems inanimate is really alive—everything in the universe is made up of molecules, which consist of atoms that are constructed of protons, neutrons and electrons. These individual components of life all interact in perfect order to keep everything in the universe together—a chair or car or a building, all in physical harmony.

Taking his cue from the interactions of life at its most basic level, Adam began to reach out to give as well as to receive. At first this was difficult for Adam because in the past he had been hurt many times by others to whom he had given. But he realized that shutting down and not giving of himself emotionally and not spending time with his wife and children resulted in strained relationships.

Adam's journey led him to seek the grace of Jesus to forgive those who had hurt him in the past. That process allowed him the freedom to give again. As he started giving and receiving love, appreciation, respect and acceptance, he began to build a meaningful and fulfilling relationship with his family. His wife later commented that her husband was more loving and caring, and had begun to do something he had rarely done before: share his life with her. Likewise, the children expressed how they loved him and how happy they were that he was a part of their lives again. They felt as if they were *as* important—if not more so—than his job.

Adam felt the time, money and effort it took him to become a meaningful husband and father in Christ was more than worth it. Most of all he praised and thanked God for revealing to him what was wrong and helping him through Jesus to put his faith into action. He discovered that God resists the proud but gives grace to the humble (see 1 Pet. 5:5). Thank God he didn't let pride get in the way.

Receiving Grace, Giving Grace

Grace works in a similar fashion. God gives us His grace that we might receive it and give it to others. This is the secret of the universe.

DIAGRAM IV

Giving and Receiving in Relationships

What makes for a healthy self-esteem? The following will help to answer this question. Think of this as a bicycle wheel. The stronger the spokes of the wheel are, the stronger the wheel is. The same holds true for the development of a healthy self-esteem. The stronger the spokes are of love, appreciation, and so forth, the stronger and healthier is your self-esteem.

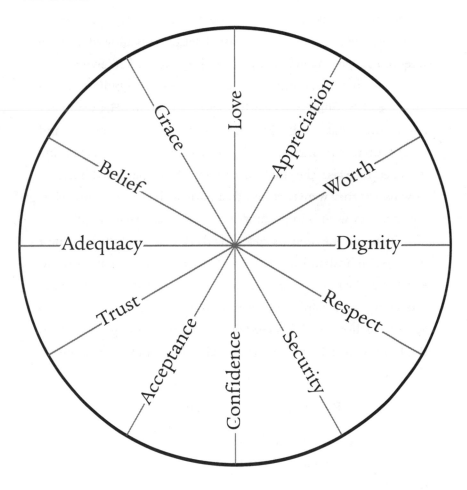

DIAGRAM IV continued

In order to determine how healthy your self-esteem is, do the following exercise. On a scale of 1 to 10 (1 being the least and 10 being the most), reflect on each spoke in terms of how strongly it affects how much you give (G) and receive (R) in all of your relationships. Rate how you see yourself in this, and then rate how you give and receive from people in your life such as a husband/wife, children, mother, father, and others.

	Self	Other		Husband/ Wife		Children (name each child)		Mother		Father	
	Now	G	R	G	R	G	R	G	R	G	R
1. Love											
2. Appreciation											
3. Worth											
4. Dignity											
5. Respect											
6. Security											
7. Confidence											
8. Acceptance											
9. Trust											
10. Belief/Faith											
11. Adequacy											
12. Grace											

When you do the exercise, there are a few spiritual principles that are evident, such as:

- Luke 6:38: "Give and it will be given to you; good measure, pressed down, shaken together, running over, will be put into your lap. For the measure you give will be the measure you get" (*RSV*) (Secret of the Universe).

- Acts 20:35: "It is more blessed to give than to receive" (*KJV*).

- Galatians 6:7: "A man reaps what he sows" (*NIV*).

- Matthew 6:21: "For where your treasure is, there will your heart be also" (*KJV*).

DIAGRAM V

A Healthy Self

Check your attitude. Is it a selfish attitude or a loving attitude (i.e., are you aware of saying things like, "If I do this for you, what are you going to do for me?")? Scriptures tell us that "God is love" (1 John 4:8). If the love of God is truly in you, you'll be able to give it away to others, but you cannot give love unless you have that treasure in your heart. Spiritual well-being, therefore, is expressed through a healthy self-love that will, in turn, be manifested in relationship with others. We demonstrate it here in the following "self" wheel:

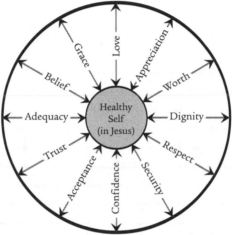

The healthy "self" wheel can be best understood in this way: A wheel that has spokes is strong as long as the spokes are strong and sturdy. "Self" can be healthy and giving if the spokes of love, appreciation, worth, and so forth, are vital, alive and feeding into "self." To put it another way, think of self as the heart and the arteries of the heart as love, appreciation, worth, and so forth. The healthier the arteries, the healthier the heart. If the arteries have any blockage or start to become hardened, this adversely affects the heart. In the same way, the healthier the arteries of love, appreciation, worth, etc., the healthier the "self."

If these arteries of love, etc., are blocked by hurt, rejection, anger, etc., then grace through Jesus in us needs to be administered to bring the healing of that artery so that it can once again flow by giving and receiving. In this way the secret of the universe is activated.

"Give, and it will be given to you. A good measure, pressed down, shaken together, and running over, will be poured into your lap. For with the measure you use, it will be measured to you" (Luke 6:38).

Jesus wants us to be one with Him and the Father. He wants us to love Him and one another. Jesus wants us to receive His grace and through Him to give it to others.

Many people, however, continue to say no to Him and His grace for their healing. The grace that is available to save our souls from eternal death and judgment is the same grace that is able to preserve our families and all the relationships so dear to us. We need to learn to walk in that grace, to appropriate the grace that is available to us in our daily interactions. As Paul said to Timothy, "You then, Timothy, my child, be strong in the grace we have in Christ Jesus" (2 Tim. 2:1, NCV).

What is keeping you from receiving and giving that grace?

Begin by acknowledging your need for grace—only then can you receive it. Grace is the free gift of forgiveness, love, mercy, unmerited favor from God through Jesus Christ. Now, as a new creature in Christ, you can give through Jesus what you have received—grace (see 2 Cor. 12:9). The next step is to give that grace to others, but giving can be difficult if receiving is a struggle. You can only give what you have already received.

In this chapter, we hope you'll engage with us in the process of receiving and giving grace, otherwise known as *forgiveness*.

The Process of Receiving and Giving

Before engaging in the process of forgiveness, it's important to count the costs. "Fixing" relationships of any kind can be complex. If you want to establish a home-building business, you count the costs of the items you'll need to accomplish the goal, which is to build homes. These costs may include permits, attorney fees, financing, subcontractors, place of business, and so on. Unfortunately, it's not that easy or straightforward with relationships. Communication is complex!

Brad was a problem teenager. His father's name was Roy, and his stepmother was Alice. Brad had little relationship with his parents beyond living with them. Communication had broken down and their relationships were strained to the breaking point. Something had to give. Sound familiar?

Despite his disrespectful attitude toward his parents, Brad desired a more meaningful relationship with them. Roy and Alice wanted a better relationship, too, but had become rigid and dictatorial in their parenting style. Even though they were Christians, they lacked grace in this area. When our faith in God becomes "religious," resulting in rules and regulations to be followed absolutely, we rarely find grace or comfort in our relationships with God or with others. It becomes a constant effort for us to be good in the eyes of God, and we never feel we measure up. Rather than walking in grace, we succumb to a religion of works that causes us to become more and more fixated on our own flaws and the shortcomings of others. We must remember that Jesus came to bring grace and to destroy the works of the enemy—and graceless religion is one of the greatest deceptions of the devil.

Jesus demonstrated a disdain for religion and its leaders, for they ushered in rules and regulations that were placed above the needs of people. Jesus, in contrast, put His relationship with the Father first and the needs of people above man-made legalism (see Matt. 12:1-14; 20:28).

Brad felt he never measured up to the legalistic expectations of his parents.

Did he smoke? No.

Did he drink? No.

Did he do drugs? No.

Did he use foul language? No.

Yet his parents could not see his positive qualities because they weren't looking at their son through eyes of grace—they were looking at him through eyes of perfectionism and religion. And they found what they were looking for: his imperfections. Remember, we find what we are looking for and what we focus on enlarges. If we look for a person's shortcomings, weaknesses, faults and sins, we'll find them.

I encouraged Brad's parents to look for and acknowledge his positive qualities. As they did so, their relationship improved. Roy and Alice began to look at Brad through eyes of grace, hear him with ears of grace, speak to him with tongues of grace, and relate to him with hearts of grace. They could forgive him for his negative actions. Grace looks for the good, the positive, the potential. Grace fosters forgiveness.

They made the first step toward a new relationship. They gave grace; it was up to Brad to respond and give his parents the grace they needed from him.

Brad noted the change in Roy and Alice, but he continued to relate to them in anger. Self got in the way. Rather than focus on what was happening in the present, Brad focused on himself and the past. Sometimes he raged against Alice because of his unrealistic desire to have his parents reconciled. This created difficulty with Alice and his father as well, and a vicious cycle continued.

Finally Brad began to see the problem was *his own anger*. By exploring his life, it became clear to him that he was angry about his father and mother divorcing. This is a common source of anger among children from broken homes. Divorce is an issue!

As Brad began to see grace as a gift of God's unconditional love and forgiveness (see diagram VI on page 198), he could begin to forgive (an act of the will) his natural parents as well as his stepmother. From the Lord's Prayer, he began to focus on the phrase "forgive us our sins as we forgive those who have sinned against us" (Matt. 6:12, NCV). He saw that in order to be forgiven, he had to extend forgiveness. He gave grace, just as he was receiving grace from his parents.

The result? Brad put Ephesians 4:32 into practice and he became more tender-hearted toward his stepmother. He forgave his parents and became more respectful toward them all. He was able to extend grace to them concerning their divorce and his father's remarriage. What kind of relationship did giving and receiving grace create? It led to mutual forgiveness, understanding, respect, appreciation, love, caring and sharing. It created an environment of harmony, one with less stress and strain.

The "Doers of Reconciliation" Process

Sharon brought her 83-year-old mother, Linda, in for counseling. Linda was so depressed that she wanted to die. She was losing weight and had many illnesses, but they couldn't discover the physical source. As we talked, we discovered that a bitter root of unforgiveness was growing inside her and literally consuming her physically. Linda had been hurt by many people in her life; people she'd never really forgiven. She didn't know if she wanted to deal with all this hurt.

I (Larry) decided to take Linda and Sharon through the following process. I asked them to carefully consider and pray about forgiveness, as people have a tendency to go through a pseudo-intellectual type of forgiveness, but never really deal with the hurt, pain, rejection and anger. Then true forgiveness—as we have been forgiven by God—could be offered.

I call this "Doers of Reconciliation," a plan I believe is from the Holy Spirit.

1. Recognize we are new creatures in Christ, old things are passed away (including the hurt, pain and rejections of the past) and all things become new as we forgive as we have been forgiven (see 2 Cor. 5:17).

2. Through Jesus as Lord of our life (past, present and future), we can forgive our deepest hurts, pain and rejections from others (see Gal. 2:20).

3. As 2 Corinthians 5:18 affirms, now we can be reconciled to God the Father. He forgives us through grace. We no longer have a religion, but a relationship with the Father through Jesus Christ.

4. Now with Jesus as Lord, we can give the same gift Jesus has given us—grace, the gift of unconditional love and forgiveness (see Matt. 20:28; Eph. 2:8).

The gift of grace isn't to be taken lightly, but rather cherished. As we give this grace to one another, we experience healing

DIAGRAM VI

Doers of Reconciliation

2 Corinthians 5:17-18   2 Corinthians 12:9
Ephesians 2:4-8   Philippians 3:13-14

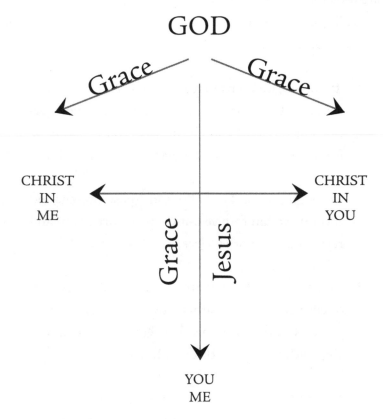

"GRACE" is a GIFT of unconditional

and

Love   **Forgiveness**
1 John 4:7-18   Matthew 6:12-15
1 Corinthians 13   Mark 11:22-26
John 15:1-12   Ephesians 4:26-32

from the past and freedom to enjoy the future. This can be true in every one of our relationships:

- Spouse to spouse
- Divorcee to divorcee
- Parent to child
- Child to parent
- Sibling to sibling
- Friend to friend
- Victim to perpetrator (see Phil. 3:13)

It does not matter if the person whom we need to forgive is dead or alive; through Jesus we can forgive as many people as we need to! We will have no closure of the past until we can forgive whoever has hurt or sinned against us.

In his book *The Gift of Forgiveness* (see diagram VII), Dr. Charles Stanley offers a wonderful, practical process for receiving and giving forgiveness:[1]

A New Heart

Isn't it exciting to know that what God said in Ezekiel 36:26 is true for you, too? "I'll give you a new heart, put a new spirit in you. I'll remove the stone heart from your body and replace it with a heart that's God-willed, not self-willed" (*THE MESSAGE*). That's Christian faith in action: not only receiving God's gift of grace but also giving it.

The Lord's Prayer lets us see the gift of grace so vividly: "Forgive us our sins, as we forgive those who have sinned against us."

DIAGRAM VII

Steps to Forgiving Others

1. Understand that forgiveness is not:
   - Justifying, understanding or explaining why the person acted toward you as he or she did.
   - Just forgetting about the offense and trusting time to take care of it.
   - Asking God to forgive the person who hurt you.
   - Asking God to forgive you for being angry or resentful against the person who offended you.
   - Denying that you were really hurt; after all, there are others who have suffered more.

2. Understand that it is often unwise to forgive face to face. This tends to make the other person feel "put down" and make you look holier-than-thou.

3. Select a time when and place where you can be alone for a while.

4. Pray and ask the Holy Spirit to bring to your mind all the people you need to forgive and the events you need to forgive them for.

5. Make a list of everything the Holy Spirit brings to your mind, even if it seems trivial to you. (Do not rush through this step—allow the Holy Spirit all the time He needs to speak to you.)

6. Take two chairs and arrange them facing each other. Seat yourself in one of the chairs.

7. Imagine that the first person on your list is sitting in the other chair. Disclose everything you can remember that the person has done to hurt you. Do not hold back the tears or the emotions that accompany the confessions.

8. Choose by an act of your will to forgive that person once and for all time. You may not feel like being forgiving. That's all right. Just do it and the feelings will follow. God will take care of that. Do not doubt what you have done is real and valid.

9. Release the person from the debt you feel is owed you for the offense. Say, "You are free and forgiven."

DIAGRAM VII continued

10. If the person is still a part of your life, now is a good time to begin accepting the individual without wanting to change aspects of his or her personality or behavior.

11. Thank the Lord for using each person as a tool in your life to deepen your insight into His grace and for conforming you to the image of His Son.

12. Pray. This is a suggested prayer to pray as you "talk" to each person: *Because I am forgiven and accepted by Christ, I can now forgive and accept you,* _____, *unconditionally in Christ. I choose now to forgive you, no matter what you did to me. I release you from the hurts* [take time to name these hurts], *and you are no longer accountable to me for them. You are free.*

13. When you have finished praying through the hurts you have suffered, pray this prayer of faith: *Lord Jesus, by faith I receive Your unconditional love and acceptance in the place of this hurt, and I trust You to meet all my needs. I take authority over the enemy, and in the name of Jesus, I take back the ground I have allowed Satan to gain in my life because of my attitude toward* _____. *Right now I give this ground back to the Lord Jesus Christ to whom it rightfully belongs.*

All this is made possible through Christ within you, who is now your Lord as well as Savior. You are made new through Jesus Christ, and the grace you received through Him, you can now give to others. Now you are free to be "kind to one another [not angry], tender hearted, [not hard hearted due to anger], forgiving one another as Jesus has forgiven you" (Eph. 4:32, *AMP*).

Jesus explained this phrase to His disciples so that they and we might understand clearly: "Yes, if you forgive others their sins, your Father in heaven will also forgive you for your sins. But if you don't forgive others, your Father in heaven will not forgive your sins" (Matt. 6:12,14-15, *NCV*). Jesus makes it clear that God the Father does not want His children imprisoned in the house that Satan built, trapped in anger, bitterness, resentment and unforgiveness. Our Father knows that these emotions will have a lasting negative effect on our lives and relationships, which in turn will nullify His grace and witness in us, ultimately turning people away from Christ.

In the Parable of the Talents, Jesus describes how the master gives talents to all, a few to some, many to others. In the story, the master was displeased with the one servant who buried his talent instead of using it (see Matt. 25:14-30). The result? The lone talent the unrighteous servant had was given to one who had the most, the one who had doubled the talents given to him. Could it be that the Father expects us not to bury the gift of grace that He has given us, but rather to give this grace freely, just as we have received it? When Jesus returns, what will He be looking for in us as the Body and Bride of Christ? Will He not be looking for how we multiplied the gift of grace that He gave us?

When Sharon and her mother, Linda, returned for a second session, they had both given this process for receiving/giving grace a lot of prayer and thought. Linda was close to dealing with the pain of the past, and proceeded over several weeks to forgive several people who had greatly hurt her. Although Linda did not want to go through the details of her hurts and rejections with me, with the help of Jesus she was able to do so.

Not only was Linda able to give grace and forgiveness, but Sharon too was convicted of the need to forgive several people in her life. Both Sharon and Linda spoke of having a peace and joy such as they had never known before. Linda, the woman who had lost all interest in life and wanted to die, now had a smile on her face. She was eating better and, most important, embracing the new life Christ had given her. The burden of anger, bitterness and resentment was removed from her shoulders and given to the Lord. She was free to enjoy life and praise Jesus for what He had done to release her.

The "List"

I (Larry) grew up in Springfield, Illinois, in the 1930s during the Depression. It was a very challenging time for many, especially our family. Our father died when I was four—I had eight older brothers and sisters, and only my youngest sister was still in the home.

Despite my mother's heavy load, whenever I was faced with a problem, she always encouraged, "You can do it, son, you can do it." The encouragement helped me at the time, but it also contributed to an ego as big as Texas, which got in the way of Christ being Lord of my life. We may not consciously understand the subtle stresses and strains of life that lead to disappointment, fear, rejection, or, in my case, perfectionism and a need to please people, but these stresses and strains can nevertheless impact our subconscious mind. My mother's over-affirmation was the first factor on the "list."

When my father died, there was no insurance money, so on top of the emotional trauma of losing our father, the financial strain on the household was incredible. Mother was eventually able to find work that paid $15 per month. The house payment alone was $25 per month, so all of us had to find ways to make money. In those days that meant having a paper route, even though I was only four. My father's failure to provide for us found a place on the "list."

As time passed and we continued our struggle to survive, I met an older boy named Clement. Clement was still in the sixth grade at the age of 16, growing up in a home in which he was beaten and rejected by his father. He developed into a rough young man who could fight. His independence and routine abuse led him to leave school at 16 years old to try to make it on his own. We became friends, and Clement became my self-appointed bodyguard. Though he was the neighborhood bully, I extended grace to him, and Clement responded with grace as he became my protector.

Clement eventually ran into problems with the law and was incarcerated for manslaughter. His temper and pent-up anger stemmed from resentment toward his father. He never forgave his father, and it cost him dearly. Such is the case for anyone who fails to deal with anger.

Twenty years went by before I saw Clement again, at a school reunion. I saw a rugged man running toward me—I did not know if I should run and hide or embrace the man! When he got close, I realized the gargantuan figure was Clement. My old bodyguard put a big bear hug on me, nearly crushing my ribs.

"Larry, it's so good to see you again," cried Clement, clinging to me like a super-magnet on steel.

"You too," I replied, out of breath.

As I reflected on this reunion, I realized the tremendous impact that grace had on the troubled young man with whom I had been friends.

I had many father figures. One was my grade-school principal, who sexually abused me when I was about eight years old. Miraculously, this event did not destroy my life, but rather caused me to seek out the love of God in Christ. It became another opportunity for me to appropriate grace and forgiveness toward a sexual predator and pedophile—but the principal joined the "list." Times of trial and stress sometimes lead to anger, bitterness and resentment, especially when people use or abuse you.

When I turned 13, I was employed by a man named Tom, who ran a heating and air conditioning (HAC) business. I was hired on a part-time basis to find potential customers, whose names could then be passed on to salesmen. I was so eager to please and be successful that between the ages of 13 to 18, I knocked on doors in 37 communities. When my brother-in-law died (who had also worked for the company), I took his place as sales manager and received training at the Williamson Heating and Air Conditioning School. I was the youngest student ever to attend, and I was highly sought after by Williamson.

Their ongoing interest in me was quite surprising, considering the persecution I underwent at the HAC. Tom, my supervisor at HAC, was a troubled man by most standards. He was a user, an adulterer, a carouser and a drunkard—the latter a habit that would eventually cost him an early grave and a departure marked by self-deceit, abuse and dishonor.

Tom made up for his inadequacies by riding the back of his sales manager—me. When I sold $50,000 in a month, Tom wanted

$75,000. When I sold $100,000, Tom wanted more. Finally after one of Tom's ridiculous demands, I finally blew up. I had enough of the abuse, the criticism, the persecution and the crumbs. I shouted and even cried—*me*, the diminutive Larry, the overachiever Larry, the man-pleaser Larry, the never-say-a-harsh-word-about-anyone Larry. Oddly, my blow-up was the turning point where Tom started to back off and to accept and respect me.

Tom, nonetheless, had injured me. So he too was added to the "list."

At 19 years of age, I was now a youth minister to 2,500 inner-city youth, as well as working part-time at the HAC. This was in addition to going to college—the first in my family to accomplish that goal. As the youngest child of the family, I was a strong achiever, though I had one brother who worked for the A&P grocery chain and was considered rich by my family. When it became clear to my family that I was going into the ministry and would be attending college, they put pressure on me to take care of my mother. This pressure increased as Mother aged. Despite the fact that there were four sisters and one other living brother (and no one else was juggling school and work), I was instructed to take care of our mother.

This made me angry, and the anger boiled over during a conversation with my brother. We were discussing my mother's situation, and my brother became distant and indifferent to my concerns about going to college, being in ministry and trying to care for Mother. He acted as if it was none of his concern, and I was outraged that my own brother should have such disregard for our mother. We almost came to blows, but God's grace carried me through.

My brother and sisters were added to the "list."

I met and married Kim shortly thereafter, continuing to work, study and pastor. Of course, this had its anticipated result on our relationship. She was terribly lonely and sought the company of men, many men, from all races and socio-economic backgrounds. If they were available, she was willing. She also suffered from mental illness, including depression and schizophrenia, resulting in acute psychotic episodes.

It was five to six years into our marriage before I discovered the inevitable: I found Kim in bed with one of her counselors. Later, she became pregnant by another man with whom she was having an adulterous relationship. I accepted Janette, the baby girl, as my own, but the marriage could not last. When Janette was just a year old, Kim and I filed for divorce. I gave little Janette to her father to adopt and raise as his own.

Kim had hurt me deeply, more than any human being I had confronted in my life. I thought I would die and felt I could never love again. My ex-wife went to the top of the "list."

One year later, I met Carol, the joy of my life to this day. A series of "coincidences" brought us together. (That's another story!) About that time, I found out that Tom, my old HAC supervisor was dying, in the hospital with alcohol-related illnesses. He wanted to see me.

It was 1962 and I was in graduate school at Washington University in St. Louis, working on my master's degree in social work. The last thing on my mind was to drive to Illinois to see an old boss who had abused me for so many years. But I left within 30 minutes of the call.

When I got to the hospital room, Tom tried to sit up in bed and give me a hug.

"Don't get up, Tom. I see you're hurting."

"Larry, I want to. Come here, please." As we hugged, tears rolled down Tom's face.

"Larry, I am so glad you came. Would you pray with me? I want to receive Jesus." We prayed the sinner's prayer, and immediately Tom died.

He was no longer on the "list."

Although consciously I felt that I never held a grudge against anyone on the "list," subconsciously I knew there were people in my life whom I needed to forgive if I was ever to receive freedom from anger, bitterness and resentment. Even after many years of research and helping others find grace, it was only during the preparation of this book that I became aware of why I needed to give and receive grace.

I had to forgive my mother for being over-protective, my father for dying and leaving me alone, my brother and sisters for their blatant disregard for our mother's welfare, my grade-school principal for sexually abusing me, Tom for taking advantage of me, and most of all, my ex-wife for cheating on me.

Grace forgives when you are alone, abused, verbally assaulted, persecuted, spit on, taken advantage of and cheated on. When a man has nothing left, nothing to hold on to, when he has destroyed himself inside and out and left a mess of his loved ones and friends, there is always someone to call. Grace will respond when the call comes. Grace will prevail. This is the prayer I prayed:

Lord Jesus, You were the one who gave me grace when I was a sinner. Lord, You died that I should live. You took all of my sins on Your back and gave me all of Your righteousness before the Father.

I did nothing but receive Your grace and forgiveness. I could do nothing but say yes to You. I heard Your voice as one calling for me to come out and walk with You. You sought me out when I was still a self-centered, ugly person, unworthy of anything. In the midst of my pursuits of fame and glory, riches and pleasure, You chose me.

You chose me. There was nothing in me of value to anyone, least of all the most Holy God of the Universe. The One true God, the righteous judge, the great I AM, the One who is and was and is to come, the One who sits in unapproachable light, the Bread of Life, the Fountain of Living Water, the Good Shepherd, but most important, my Lord and Savior.

You saved me from my sins.

You released me from the prison of my addictions.

You delivered me from anger and lust.

You helped me to forgive myself, my spouse, my family and others, Lord.

I received Your grace, and now I can give it as well.

CHAPTER 9

Building Bridges of
Reconciliation

Michigan is unique among states in our country. Aside from having one of the best perennial hockey teams, the Detroit Red Wings, and the greatest concentration of fresh water in the entire world, Michigan is split into two land masses. The lower land mass is referred to as the Lower Peninsula (LP) and the upper land mass is the Upper Peninsula (UP). There is a physical separation between the two groups of people, and there is a separation of cultures as well.

Many in the UP feel that those from the LP really don't understand their needs or their core values. The UP is different from the LP in many ways. It is sparsely populated and very rural, with waterfalls, hills, sand dunes, undisturbed natural beauty. UP has very little to do with industrialization, other than some minerals that are mined there. In the twentieth century, there were several attempts by the UP to secede from Michigan. (These were unsuccessful.)

People used to travel between the UP and the LP by ferry until they built a bridge along the Straits of Mackinac (pronounced MACK-in-aw). Many envisioned a bridge as far back as the 1880s. Back then a store owner in St. Ignace published a newspaper advertisement that included an artist's portrayal of the Brooklyn Bridge with the caption "Proposed bridge across the Straits of Mackinac."

In 1934, the Michigan Legislature created the Mackinac Straits Bridge Authority to study the feasibility of the bridge and authorized it to sell bonds for the project. Preliminary plans for the bridge featured a three-lane roadway, a railroad crossing on the under deck of the span, and a center-anchorage double-suspension bridge configuration similar to the design of the

San Francisco-Oakland Bay Bridge. From 1939 to 1941, a causeway of approximately 4,000 feet in length was constructed with concrete road fragments extending from the northern shore. With uncertainty in funding and the initiation of World War II, further building was delayed. In 1950, engineers resumed construction and the state legislature authorized the sale of $85 million in construction bonds on April 30, 1952.

David B. Steinman was appointed the design engineer in January 1953, and the American Bridge Division of United States Steel Corporation was awarded a contract of over $44 million to build the steel superstructure. On November 1, 1957, after two-and-a-half years of construction and the loss of five lives, the bridge finally opened to traffic. It was officially dedicated on June 25, 1958. The bridge is approximately five miles long, the third longest in the United States. Forty years after the dedication, the 100-millionth crossing was celebrated.

Most of us probably look at the construction of this bridge as a feat of modern engineering. True enough, it is. But behind the construction was the *need*: the need to connect two cultures and two land masses, to expand and improve economic prosperity by bringing people together.

Did the bridge spring up immediately? No.

How did it start? With a vision, a picture in the minds of visionaries of what it might resemble and how it might change the lives of all affected by its construction. When it became clear that ferries were too expensive and too inefficient to accomplish the goals of connecting the two sides, the bridge came to the forefront of everyone's mind. The old ways of transportation just were not working. Something new had to be put into place.

Was it cheap? No.

Was it easy to build? No.

Were human lives put in danger? Yes.

Was it worth the cost, the hardship, the lives lost, the requirements of years of work and commitment to make this bridge happen? For most people connected with the bridge, the answer was an overwhelming *yes*.

Counting the Cost

Like suspension bridges built across bodies of water, it takes time, money and risk for bridges of healing grace to be built between estranged people. Many may feel that the cost is too high to achieve the bridge. It might cost me time or pride. I might have to say I'm sorry. What if the person to whom I am trying to direct my bridge of grace laughs at me, scorns me or refuses my overture—or worse yet, just plain ignores me?

Jesus says that we must count the costs of discipleship (see Luke 14:28). Building bridges of grace that result in restored relationships is probably one of the most important costs of being a disciple of Jesus. Christ taught that reconciled relationships are more important to God than any offering we could bring before Him: "Therefore if you bring your gift to the altar, and there remember that your brother has something against you, leave your gift there before the altar, and go your way. First be reconciled to your brother, and then come and offer your gift" (Matt. 5:23-24, *NKJV*).

Why? Because for God, how we treat others is synonymous with how we treat Him: "If someone says, 'I love God,' and hates his brother, he is a liar; for the one who does not love his brother whom he has seen, cannot love God whom he has not seen" (1 John 4:20).

Building bridges of grace for reconciliation is the most important act in the kingdom of God. Let's look at it another way:

> You're blessed when you can show people how to cooperate instead of compete or fight. That's when you discover who you really are, and your place in God's family (Matt. 5:9, *THE MESSAGE*).

The *New International Version* states, "Blessed are the peacemakers, for they shall be called sons of God." Can you think of any more profound title than "sons (or daughters) of God"?

Jennifer's Story

Jennifer was married to a driven man named Jordan who had been married several times. Jennifer knew that Jordan had very few family relationships left intact because over the years his hard-nosed personality had grated against others and driven them away.

When he was diagnosed with advanced colon cancer, Jennifer felt that it was time to build some bridges. She began by asking, "Jordan, when was the last time you spoke to your sister, Veronica?"

"Oh, about 10 years," he replied.

"Why?"

Jordan thought for a minute, and then said, "Honey, I don't know."

Not wanting to let him off the hook, Jennifer kept prodding him until he thought back to the last time he spoke with his sister.

"Well," Jordan started, "I gave her a 1-800 number so she could call me . . ."

"Go on," Jennifer prompted.

"Okay. I gave her the number so she could call me to discuss how her son was getting along working for me in the warehouse business. Veronica called me one Tuesday and I was very short with her because I was so busy. You know how busy I get on Tuesdays." By this time Jordan was feeling defensive.

"So you gave Veronica a special number to call you. She called you about her son, Billy, and you blew her off like she was some kind of cheap salesman. Is that it?"

By this time Jordan was quite defensive and unwilling to continue.

Jennifer called Veronica and spent a good amount of time on the phone with her, going over the hurts of the past.

"I remember that conversation like it was yesterday," Veronica explained. "I was just trying to find out how Billy was doing on the job, and Jordan treated me like I didn't exist. I felt I was worthless, or at least that was how he made me feel." She began to cry.

Thanks to Jennifer, who acted as a peacemaker and bridgebuilder, the once-estranged sister had the opportunity to see her terminally ill brother.

Did Jordan ever admit to being wrong in this case? Unfortunately, no. He was too proud for that—but because of the persistence of his sensitive wife, she was able to build a bridge of grace with Jordan's sister, resulting in the restoration of the relationship. Would Jordan have benefited from admitting his fault? Undoubtedly, yes. Jordan brought estrangement to his relationship with his sister and never asked for forgiveness. Instead, he settled for the opportunity to converse with his sister before his death.

Jordan's daughter, Caitlyn, was a replica of her German father—proud, uncompromising and self-centered. She found it hard to reconcile with others, therefore making her a difficult person with whom to relate.

When Caitlyn found out her father had terminal colon cancer, she took the opportunity to write him a nasty hate-note chronicling the years of disappointment, anger, bitterness and resentment that she had kept bottled inside of her. Jennifer read the letter first and was horrified. Instead of letting Jordan read it, she wrote Caitlyn a six-page letter telling her what a good man her father had become. Jennifer recognized that Caitlyn's angry letter, though justified, was not appropriate because of Jordan's terminal illness.

"Your father is dying. You have the opportunity to put away your anger and hatred toward him, and realize that he cares for you deeply. I will not allow you to maintain the severance of this relationship because I care enough about you to help you see the need for reconciliation before his death. You need to know that your father loves you with all of his heart."

Her mother's input helped. Caitlyn began to take her eyes off herself and to realize that her opportunity to restore the relationship with her father was time-limited. The time was passing quickly and she had to make a decision, or by default lose the knowledge of his love for her forever.

As a third party, it wasn't Jennifer's direct relationships she was trying to repair, yet she could step back and see how important her investment of time and energy would be in building that bridge of grace. She was sensitive to the fact that her husband was abrasive, yet she knew that beyond the hard exterior, he really wanted to be able to communicate love to his family—especially now at a time when he was facing eternity. Jennifer sets a great example as we consider how to build bridges of grace for reconciliation.

Frank's Story
Frank's wife gave him an ultimatum: Get counseling or get out.

Perhaps the pride in many men would make it too much for them to acquiesce to this kind of demand from a wife, but because Frank loved his wife and children deeply, he put his pride aside and regarded her demand as a wakeup call. He responded immediately.

What led his wife, Katrina, to this point of desperation?

Frank was doing something to his family that he detested and in his shame never thought he would ever do. He both physically and verbally abused them. Although it's no excuse, he grew up being badly beaten by his father. At the age of 15, Frank could take it no longer and ran away from home, never to return. Because he was physically mature, he got a job and through hard work and determination he was able to make it on his own. What he previously attributed to his own abilities and self-made manhood, he now realizes was the grace of God.

He was 40 years old at the time he came for counseling. He'd become a successful businessman, yet for all of his achievements he was paralyzed by (and bitterly ashamed of) his abusive behavior. As a result of his guilt and seeming inability to control his anger, he considered suicide. He called Focus on the Family and was referred to me (Larry) for counseling.

Over the phone, he agreed to come for counseling three times per week even though he lived about 200 miles away. He was determined to overcome his personal problems with the same intensity and passion that helped him become the success he was in business. Unlike some, he recognized that his abuse of his wife and children was unacceptable and that he had to find a better way of dealing with his explosive anger before it was too late.

As Frank and I explored his anger, it became clear that it was the result of unresolved anger he had toward his abusive father. His rage and disdain were so intense that when I suggested that he needed to forgive his father in order to be set free, his response was emphatic: "If you were my father and I had a knife, I'd stab you a thousand times, and it wouldn't be enough!"

During our first two counseling sessions, when I shared what I thought Frank should do, he got up and walked out the door, not indicating if he would return. He later called for another appointment. During the third session, I didn't change the subject or water down the medicine, and he was finally ready to receive it. He listened and responded positively to what he needed to do to overcome and heal his anger. He realized that he needed to be a "doer of reconciliation" and go through steps to forgiveness. I encouraged him to pray about what he needed to do to complete the grace process, to build a bridge of grace that would lead to reconciliation with his wife and children.

Like anyone else who has an anger problem, Frank had to learn to deal appropriately with the past. He said, "Either I deal with the anger, or anger will deal with me." Anger can control behavior, especially in relationships, consciously or unconsciously. In Frank's case it was unconscious; the last thing he consciously wanted to do was to hurt his wife and children. Anger is like pressing a spring down: You can press it down only so far, and when you let go, it springs up out of control. When you press anger down, it turns from anger to resentment to bitterness to hostility to hatred, exploding along the way. The more anger is suppressed and stuffed internally, the more out of control it is when it's eventually expressed. And when the anger is not addressed daily, it can result in depression, commonly referred to as "anger turned inward." We must make a choice: Deal with anger or have it will deal with us.

Frank chose to deal with his. He no longer wanted to give an opportunity to Satan by letting the sun go down on his anger (see Eph. 4:26-27). He determined that he must deal with the issues surrounding his father; so on the way home he bought a baseball bat and drove out into the country, stopping at a pasture. He got out of the car and found the biggest tree he could find, which became, in his mind, his father. Following steps five and six in the process of forgiveness, Frank beat the bat against the tree to express his anger. When his anger was spent, he began to build a bridge of grace and forgive his father. The visible bruises on his hand were a testament to the beginnings of what could not be seen, the healing of his scarred heart.

The change in Frank's heart was evident immediately. He recognized that anger, bitterness and resentment toward his father was being directed to everyone he loved. Only through the grace and love of the Lord Jesus Christ was this possible for him to realize, and he praised the Lord for helping him deal with his anger and build a bridge of grace for reconciliation.

Weeks later, Frank and his family came to the office. His wife, Katrina, spoke of how their relationship had been restored because of the bridge of grace God had built in Frank's life. As a result of his new attitude, and the freedom he received from his past hurts and pent-up anger, Katrina was able to forgive Frank and embrace the grace that the Lord wanted to bring to her and the kids. Our session closed with their five-year-old hugging my legs, saying, "Thanks for giving me a new dad."

Mary and Rick's Story

Mary and Rick are a couple who recently struggled with the issue of pornography. Two years into their marriage, they realized that they desperately needed to find a bridge of grace to bring reconciliation to their marriage.

Pornography is an addiction that affects many men—it is an escape. Even though Mary and Rick thought they had a sexually intimate and satisfying relationship, Rick got pulled into the pit of this trap. Mary viewed Rick's addiction with disdain and disgust. She believed it was akin to having an adulterous affair.

Finally the two came in for counseling. Rick had realized for some time that his preoccupation with pornography was controlling his mind, his motivation and his time. Like a vice-grip around his heart and mind, soon it would squeeze the spiritual life out of him. The Lord warns, "Watch over your heart with all diligence for from it flow the issues of life" (Prov. 4:23).

As a born-again Christian and deacon in his church, Rick felt relieved when his wife (who worked with youth at their church) found out about the problem and confronted him. (In general we suggest that women actively address this problem by confronting their husbands and holding them accountable as Mary did. Once the secret is no longer a secret, the power of the enemy to hold judgment over the man lessens and the issue can be dealt with appropriately.)

At this point Rick realized that he had a major problem, that he needed to respond to his wife honestly and that he needed help to repair the damage he'd brought to their relationship. Yet he also needed grace, and his wife needed to give him that grace if their marriage was to recover from this devastating addiction.

Mary gave grace through her willingness to attend the counseling sessions and look at herself as possibly contributing to her husband's addiction. Rick responded in grace by taking the blame and not trying to place it on his wife. He took full responsibility. This give-and-take encouraged them as they worked toward the common goal of improving their sexual intimacy, and in turn, their marriage.

As Mary began to understand the cause of her husband's insecurities and the source of his pain, it was easier for her to give grace and forgiveness and to love him unconditionally through the healing process. This is grace in action.

Did Rick deserve grace or forgiveness? No.

Did Mary give it anyway? Yes.

And the result? Healing for these hurting people and their hurting marriage. As a result of Mary's outpouring of grace, Rick found the motivation and encouragement to want a deeper and more intimate relationship with God and his wife.

While Rick went through Rapha's 12-step guide for sexual addiction, the couple also worked on building bridges of grace based on the author of grace, Jesus (see Titus 3:5). This strong bridge of grace created a platform across which they could safely and securely walk and talk, share and discover each other's needs and resolve issues and conflicts while learning, growing and changing together with Christ in the center. Although they had been married less than two years, the exercise of their faith and the grace they shared demonstrated a greater maturity than many long-married couples seen in counseling.

They both discovered they had let anger build up in their lives concerning issues they had never managed effectively. Rick discovered that the anger he had toward unaffectionate parents, who fought often and loved little, was now suppressed to the point where his inner turmoil was being temporarily satisfied by the pleasure of escapism. This trap door of pornography allowed Satan to come in, establish a foothold and begin to destroy the thing he hates most: people and relationships. But God had another plan, and by the power of forgiveness and His grace, He restored this couple and made them stronger than ever.

Rick did not intend to hurt Mary, but she was hurt nonetheless. Note that Rick's obsession with sexual stimuli had nothing to do with his wife. It was about anger that had been bottled up inside and needed to be dealt with by grace and forgiveness. You may want to keep this in mind as you refer back to the steps to forgiving others (see diagram VII in chapter 8)—sometimes when people hurt us, their motivations have nothing to do with us.

Bruce's Story

Bruce was an alcoholic. He and his wife, Hilda, had tried everything to free him, but nothing had worked. Hilda came for counseling, having all but given up on her husband and their marriage. She had no hope, but realized she needed help. The idea that her husband might come in for counseling seemed unlikely. The thought of her children was the only other motivator for her to seek help for their marriage.

Hilda attended a few counseling sessions and began to realize that she was part of the problem, not the solution. She was an enabler, allowing Bruce to carry on without accountability. Eventually she gained the courage to confront him with his problem. To her amazement, he agreed to counseling. When they, along with their children, came for counseling, Bruce shared how he had felt rejected from the time of his youth.

As he related story after story about his history of rejection, Hilda and the three boys (nine-year-old twins and one four-year-old) listened intently. They saw their 300-pound husband and father cry like a baby. Their heartstrings were touched as Bruce opened up emotionally about his past. Their response was spontaneous and overwhelmingly meaningful to Bruce.

One of the twins hugged his dad and crawled up on his lap as he said, "Dad, I sure love you." The other twin immediately followed suit. With the twins now sitting on his lap, one on one leg, one on the other, the four-year-old raced toward Bruce and jumped up in the middle of all three. He hugged his father's neck and said, "Boy, Dad, I sure do love you!"

Again the stream of tears came running down his face, as he hugged all three boys. His wife was the last to respond. He would not forget what she said.

"Honey," she cried joyfully, "you can see that we all forgive you and love you very much."

What healing grace took place! Bruce needed a bridge of grace to open the door for healing in his life. He began to see how much his family loved and accepted him. He recognized that he had been escaping into alcohol as an adult to cover up the rejection he experienced as a young person. As he visualized what he was missing in his family life he made a commitment to the Lord and his family never to touch another drop of alcohol again.

All too often, turning to alcohol or some other addiction is actually an escape from something of which we are afraid. Many times it's fear of not being loved or accepted, not measuring up or being rejected. Satan deceives us here because the escape ultimately brings about the thing we are most afraid of—rejection.

A few months after our counseling ended, Bruce called with enthusiasm in his voice. He wanted me to know that he was having the time of his life. They were on their first family vacation and attending a major league baseball game, having a blast together. Not only had he abstained from alcohol, but he also had absolutely no desire to drink. He was so grateful to God for delivering him from alcohol addiction and turning him toward his wife and children. In his words, "Wow, I didn't know that life could be so wonderful!"

God's healing grace liberated Bruce and his family from the great escape of alcohol and enabled them to build a bridge of grace across which they could learn how to better communicate love with each other and resolve life issues and conflicts.

Here is a summary of steps to building bridges of grace for reconciliation:

1. Recognize that a problem exists. Typical inappropriate responses to life issues result in strained, dysfunctional, abusive and sometimes dissolved relationships. These responses include addictions to sex, drugs and alcohol, food, work and gambling. This usually takes time.

2. Communicate to your family or the offended party your action plan for getting qualified Christian counseling for the problem.

3. Discover and deal with the root causes of your dysfunction (e.g., anger due to early abuse, addiction to cover up insecurities and inferiority, unforgiveness, and so on).

4. Understand and appropriate the total acceptance of the love of God through Jesus Christ and His grace for you in every step of your recovery.

5. Forgive, forgive, forgive all through His marvelous and amazing grace, through which we can indeed build a bridge of grace.

Once again, we want to reiterate the six healing phrases and encourage you to make them a part of your life: "I was wrong." "You were right." "I am sorry." "I forgive you." "Please forgive me." "I love you." As you continue to read through the book, we hope these words will tie together the process of healing grace.

Revival of Reconciliation

At the end of a church seminar on Healing Grace for Hurting People, the pastor came forward and said, "I have six people I need to forgive and be forgiven by." The pastor proceeded to kneel down in front of each of these six people (all present), and first asked them to forgive him for the anger he held in his heart toward them, and then forgave them for the event that precipitated his anger. Imagine what happened when this kind of bridge of grace was constructed right in the middle of the sanctuary during the seminar on healing grace!

There wasn't a dry eye in the house. People were filled with remorse and repentance and what followed was a Holy Spirit revival of reconciliation. Spouses began to reach out to each other as did parents to children, many church members to one another. There were hugs, kisses, tears, every outpouring of the heart as the Holy Spirit moved for people present to forgive each other.

Truly God's grace abounded for reconciliation. It was an experience like none I'd ever had before at a church.

Could this be a prelude to what God wants for the Body of Christ, His Church? Could it be that the grace that saved us is the grace that now works in our relationships with other brothers and sisters in Christ? Could it be that this is why the epistles of the New Testament frequently begin and end with the word "grace"?

Just imagine. What would our world look like if the grace of the Lord Jesus flourished as it did that night in churches, couples and families? Would there be as many church splits, church hoppings, divorces, family feuds, bigotry, crime or dis-crimination? What would the world look like if Christians actually lived out the Scriptures in their lives? Others could see beyond the shadow of a doubt that Christ makes the difference and that even as we are forgiven, we too can forgive. No other religion in the world has what Christianity has to offer. We have a Savior, Jesus Christ, who saves us from our sin by grace and, through that same process, Jesus saves our marriages, fam-ilies and congregations, and heals us of hurts and rejections of the past and present.

As God reached down and built a bridge of grace through Jesus for us to be reconciled to Himself, we can reach out to each other in that same grace to reconcile ourselves to one another. This is what building bridges of grace is all about. This means appropriating healing grace in all of our relationships—past or present, dead or alive. By building bridges of grace, we can be reconciled to one another and be healed of our past. We can forget what lies behind and look forward to what lies ahead. As Philippians 3:13 reminds us, "Brothers, I do not consider myself yet to have taken hold of it. But one thing I do: Forget-ting what is behind and straining toward what is ahead."

CHAPTER 10

Preparing for the Return of the King

T he *Lord of the Rings*, written by J.R.R. Tolkien, was published on October 20, 1955. Tolkien was a contemporary of the Christian apologist and writer C. S. Lewis. This trilogy that has thrilled millions focuses on a make-believe land called Middle-earth and its mythical inhabitants, who display the spectrum of human characteristics, from deceit and treachery to bravery and self-sacrifice.

In the final book of the trilogy, called *The Return of the King*, Aragorn, the king of Gondor, returns to his rightful throne as Middle-earth is saved from the ravages of the people of Mordor. This popular story is filled with fascinating allegory and descriptive imaginative tales, some of which are similar to the return of our King, Jesus Christ. Aragorn is a strong-willed, handsome man who quietly and calmly commands the respect and loyalty of his troops. He never compromises and always leads by example and self-sacrifice.

He is likened in some respects to Jesus Christ, the King of our faith. Jesus sacrificed Himself on the cross. He sought to meet the needs of people: "For even the Son of Man did not come to be served, but to serve, and to give his life as a ransom for many" (Mark 10:45).

Unlike Aragorn, however, Jesus is a King who fought a battle that only He could fight, win and share with others. He fought the battle not over Middle-earth but over the entire earth and the people who dwell on it. Only Jesus could become the sacrifice for our sins because of His work on behalf of the entire world.

You and I fight many battles on Earth and Satan attempts to bring us down, to limit our impact and to steal our joy. He tries to keep us from experiencing the fullness of life. Yet the war has been won and Jesus accomplished it! He is the King and Lord of everything. He has the power and authority to do what is on His heart. *Our* King has chosen to give us the Kingdom (see Luke 12:32).

Now we know that the King is coming. He is returning to the earth as the rightful heir to the throne of this world. His coming is certain, although the timing is not. Look at what the Scripture says about this:

> For the coming of the son of Man will be just like the days of Noah. For as in those days which were before the flood they were eating and drinking, they were marrying and giving in marriage, until the day that Noah entered the ark, and they did not understand until the flood came and took them all away; so shall the coming of the Son of Man be. Then there shall be two men in the field; one will be taken, and one will be left. Two women will be grinding at the mill; one will be taken, and one will be left. Therefore be on the alert, for you do not know which day your Lord is coming (Matt. 24:37-42, *NASB*).

> But the day of the Lord will come like a thief, in which the heavens will pass away with a roar and the elements will be destroyed with intense heat, and the earth and its works will be burned up. Since all these things are to be destroyed in this way, what sort of people ought you to be in holy conduct and godliness? (2 Pet. 3:10-11, *NASB*).

Peter asks the question that is the point of this final chapter of the book: "What sort of people ought you and I to be in our conduct and relationships? What are we to be like as we wait for the return of the King?"

The book you've been reading is about healing grace and how that grace can help hurting people when we apply it to our relationships with our spouse, children, parents, co-workers, and so on. We've discussed that we are saved *by* grace and we are to live *by* grace (see 2 Eph. 2:8-9; Col. 2:6-7). The gift of grace results in:

1. Salvation (see John 3:16; Rom. 10:9)
2. New birth—being born again (see John 3:6)
3. New creature in Christ (see 2 Cor. 5:17)
4. The gift of the Holy Spirit (see Acts 2:38)
5. Being the adopted son/daughter of the living God (see Rom. 8:14-16)
6. Being joint heirs with Jesus (see Rom. 8:17)
7. Victory—more than conquerors through Jesus (see Rom. 8:37; 1 Cor. 15:57)
8. Daily giving up self to be crucified with Jesus (see Gal. 2:20)

We're to make use of the grace God has given us in a manner consistent with being a child of the King. His grace is greater than all our sin and the sins of those who have wronged us. We're all alike. There is nothing we have done that God cannot forgive and there is nothing anyone has done to us for which we can deny them that same gift. *This* is how we are to conduct ourselves while we wait for Jesus to return.

Albert struggled with anger and rage. It affected him in his work and in his relationship with his children, friends and extended family. He was a Christian and a leader in his church, but he felt God had let him down by allowing his wife to die of cancer and leaving him with two teenaged daughters.

He felt he needed a wife and that his children needed a step-mother. About 18 months after his wife's passing, Albert started dating a divorced woman named Janice who also had two children. They hit it off and were growing closer to one another and their children seemed to get along fine. Everything seemed to be moving along quite well when suddenly Janice dropped Albert. It came out that she had been secretly seeing another man whom she'd dated before Albert.

Albert felt betrayed. He thought that he and Janice were doing fine and he was thinking about marrying her. The situation devastated him and made him extremely angry. He started to withdraw from life, his children and his work. His depression led him to miss work. As he spiraled downward, he was finally faced with the possibility of losing his job if he didn't get help. He chose to seek out counseling, something he thought he would never do.

Discovering that he still had anger over the death of his wife, Albert first dealt with healing his grief. He began to deal with his hurt and pain and the way he blamed God for his wife's death. He worked through that issue. Then he forgave the doctors who could not heal her and even forgave her for dying and leaving him with two teenagers. He also had to forgive himself for not being the dad he knew he should be. He knew he should spend more time with his daughters rather than finding them a substitute mother. He admitted his wife had been the primary parent, but he rationalized that was all right since the children were both girls.

Albert went through the healing grace process for his wife's death but held on to his anger and resentment toward Janice. Finally after several months he concluded that he had to forgive her as well. He had started back to church with his daughters and the pastor gave a series of sermons on forgiveness. He saw that God was talking to him, so he began to work on forgiving Janice and the other man.

He said he recalled the saying, "What would Jesus do?" and was convicted of the need to forgive Janice. He said it was as if a black cloud lifted as he extended God's grace to her. He could see the sunshine of Christ for the first time in years. God restored his joy and peace. He grew closer to his daughters. He became a different man.

Through Jesus, Albert not only received God's grace but was also able to give this grace to others, including his daughters and Janice. Albert discovered what he could do by allowing Jesus to be the absolute Lord of his life.

What would Jesus say to Albert? "Well done, my faithful servant. Because you have been able to exercise grace in your life, grace will continue to abound in your life and bless you and those around you. Receive the joy of your salvation and look forward to what I have prepared for you" (see Matt. 25). God wants to be gracious to us and have compassion on us. As Scripture says, "O people in Zion, inhabitant in Jerusalem, you will weep no longer. He will surely be gracious to you at the sound of your cry; when He hears it, He will answer you" (Isa 30:19).

God is waiting on you just as you are waiting on Him. It's your move.

Could it be that Jesus will reward those who have multiplied the gift of grace to heal and reconcile their marriages, families, church fellowships and other relationships? What will Jesus do when He finds those who have received the gift of grace but who have not given this gift to those in their lives? It's a question to be considered.

It's not too late! Today you can give this gift of grace to heal and reconcile your marriage, family and other relationships. You can do what God has asked you to do—forgive—and leave the rest up to the Holy Spirit working in the others' lives through Jesus as Lord, to heal and reconcile all their relationships, especially their relationship with you.

So once again we ask, what will Jesus find when He returns? He is coming and it could be soon. Many Christians believe we are in our last days. You have received the gift of grace freely through Jesus. Now through Jesus as Lord of your life you can give this gift of grace freely. What is astounding about giving this gift of grace is that the more you give it, the more you've got it in abundance.

God wants to give us every good and perfect gift. That's what's amazing. The greatest gift of all is Jesus and His marvelous amazing grace. Now through Jesus Christ you can:

1. Give freely this gift of grace that you have received freely, so all of your past and present relationships dead or alive can be healed.

2. Be healed of your past and present hurts, disappointments and rejections from others, and healed of your anger, bitterness, resentment and unforgiveness, as you give the same gift of grace to others.

3. Follow the practical steps outlined in the previous chapters to bring healing grace, not only to all of your hurts caused by others, but also the hurts that you have caused others.

4. Let God's grace abound in your life to forgive yourself. God wants you to receive His gift of grace so that you will be blessed and be more of a blessing to others. Now your relationships can become all the more the way God intended so that His love can abound in your life.

5. Express the six relationship healing phrases: "I was wrong." "You were right." "I am sorry." "I forgive you." "Please forgive me." "I love you."

Remember, you have a blessed hope: "May the God of hope fill you with all joy and peace as you trust in Him, that you may overflow with hope, by the power of the Holy Spirit" (Rom. 15:13). Thank God that we, His adopted children, are now freed by His grace to live to His glory and praise. Could it be that this is the reason God saves us?

Our prayer is that when our King returns, He will find you healthy, whole and living in grace, ministering healing grace to a hurting world. Once we were hurting people; now we are healed. Once we were guilty people; now we are forgiven. Once we were lost and afraid, angry and empty, ashamed and imprisoned; now we are found, filled and *free* by the grace of God through Jesus Christ.

May His joy be complete in you, His love be perfected in you and His healing grace be appropriated and practiced by you everyday for the rest of your life.

Pray with us:

Lord Jesus, thank You for forgiving me for all of my sins.
Thank You for taking all of my guilt and shame,
anger and bitterness,
sorrow and rejection and nailing it with You to the cross.
Thank You for dying to give me new life.
Thank You for rising that I might have everlasting life with You.
Thank You for the free gift of Your grace,
the grace that has healed me and set me free.
Thank You for empowering me to give that grace to others.
Thank You that, in Your strength, I can genuinely forgive all those
who have hurt, offended and disappointed me.
I can love those who have abused me.
I can treat my spouse, my family, my friends,
my co-workers and others
with respect and kindness because of Your healing
grace at work within me.
Thank You for the grace to forgive myself.
Because You forgive, love and accept me, I can do the same.
Thank You for freeing me from a critical,
negative spirit and for stopping

the negative videos of fear, regret, failure and resentment
that used to replay in my mind.
Thank You for transforming my mind through Your Word.
Thank You for healing my heart.
Thank You for healing my relationships.
Thank You for a bright future ahead.
I love You, Lord Jesus.
And it's in Your Name above all names that I pray,
Amen.

ENDNOTES

Preface

1. Julia H. Johnston, "Grace Greater Than All Our Sin," first published in *Hymns Tried and True* (Chicago, IL: The Bible Institute Colportage Association, 1911).

Chapter 1: There Is Hope for You

1. All names used in this book have been changed to protect the individual's identity.

Chapter 2: What Is Healing Grace?

1. Philip Yancey, *What's So Amazing About Grace?* (Grand Rapids, MI: Zondervan, 1977), p. 70.
2. John Ortberg, *Love Beyond Reason* (Grand Rapids, MI: Zondervan, 1998), p. 139.
3. David Seamands, *Healing Grace* (Colorado Springs, CO: Victor Books, 1988), p. 115.
4. Robert S. McGee, "My Identity in Christ," *The Search for Significance* (Nashville, TN: Thomas Nelson Publishers, 2003).
5. Don Colbert, M.D., *Deadly Emotions* (Nashville, TN: Thomas Nelson, 2003), pp. 147-148.

Chapter 3: Who Is on the Throne of Your Life?

1. Adapted from Charles Solomon, *Counseling with the Mind of Christ* (Old Tappan, NJ: Fleming H. Revell, Co., 1977), p. 67.
2. Adapted from Don Colbert, M.D., *Deadly Emotions* (Nashville, TN: Thomas Nelson, 2003), pp. 25-27.
3. Ibid., p. 35.
4. Ibid., p. 64.
5. Joyce Meyer, *Battlefield of the Mind* (Nashville, TN: Warner Faith, 1995.)

Chapter 4: Are You Ready for Change?

1. Warren Wiersbe, taken from a message on "Back to the Bible" broadcast.

Chapter 5: How God's Word Changes Your Thoughts

1. David Seamands, *Healing Grace* (Colorado Springs, CO: Victor Books, 1988), adapted, pp. 61-65.
2. Les and Leslie Parrott, *Love Talk* (Grand Rapids, MI: Zondervan, 2004), adapted, p. 153.
3. Adapted from Don Colbert, M.D., *Deadly Emotions* (Nashville, TN: Thomas Nelson, 2003), pp. 156-158.
4. *Merriam-Webster's Collegiate Dictionary*, 10th ed., s.v. "slander."
5. Clifford I. Notorius and Howard J. Markman, *We Can Work It Out, How to Solve Conflicts, Save Your Marriage, and Strengthen Your Love for Each Other* (New York: GP Putnam's Sons, 1993), p. 139.
6. Notorius and Markman, pp. 144-145.
7. Max Lucado, *A Love Worth Giving* (Nashville, TN: W Publishing Group, 2002), adapted, pp. 87-88.
8. Ibid., pp. 88-89.
9. Ibid.
10. Ibid., pp. 90-91.

11. Nancy Guthrie, *The One Year Book of Hope* (Tyndale Publishers, 2005), p. 357.
12. T. W. Hunt, *The Mind of Christ* (Nashville, TN: Broadman & Holman, 1995), adapted, pp. 6-12.
13. Ibid., p. 12.
14. John Hagee, *God's Two Minute Warning* (Nashville, TN: Thomas Nelson, 2000).
15. Adapted from Colbert, *Deadly Emotions*, pp. 158-160.

Chapter 6: From Anger to Forgiveness—Grace in Action
1. Dictionary.com, s.v. "anger." http://dictionary.reference.com/browse/anger (accessed June 2007).
2. Don Colbert, MD, *Deadly Emotions* (Nashville, TN: Thomas Nelson, 2003), p. 123.
3. Michael E. McCullough, Stephen J. Sandage and Everett L. Worthington, Jr., *Forgive Is Human* (Downer's Grove, IL: IVP, 1997), p. 148.
4. Dr. Sidney B. Simon and Suzanne Simon, *Forgiveness* (New York: Warner Books, 1991), p. 43.
5. Ibid., pp. 75-76.
6. Lewis Smedes, *Forgive and Forget* (New York: Harper & Row, 1984), p. 118.
7. H. Norman Wright, *Always Daddy's Girl* (Ventura, CA: Regal Books, 1989), pp. 234-237.
8. Richard P Walters, *Anger: Yours and Mine, and What to Do About It* (Grand Rapids, MI: Zondervan, 1981), pp. 150-151.

Chapter 7: Communicating Grace
1. H. Norman Wright, *Communication: Key to Your Marriage* (Ventura, CA: Regal Books, 2000), p. 76.
2. Ibid.

Chapter 8: The Secret of the Universe
1. Charles F. Stanley, *The Gift of Forgiveness* (Nashville, TN: Thomas Nelson Publishers, 1991), appendix B, pp. 173-175.